D0331866

For Better, For Worse:

Patient in the Maelstrom

by
Carolyn Perry

For Better, For Worse: Patient in the Maelstrom
Copyright © 2011, by Carolyn Perry.
Cover photographs by Brad Loper/The Dallas
Morning News. Used by permission.
Inset photo by Barbara DeArmond

All rights reserved, including the right to reproduce this book or portions thereof in any form whatsoever. For information contact Sunbury Press, Inc., Subsidiary Rights Dept., 2200 Market St., Camp Hill, PA 17011 USA or legal@sunburypress.com.

For information about special discounts for bulk purchases, please contact Sunbury Press, Inc. Wholesale Dept. at (717) 254-7274 or orders@sunburypress.com.

To request one of our authors for speaking engagements or book signings, please contact Sunbury Press, Inc. Publicity Dept. at publicity@sunburypress.com.

FIRST SUNBURY PRESS EDITION
Printed in the United States of America
June 2011

ISBN 978-1-934597-42-2

Published by:
Sunbury Press
Camp Hill, PA
www.sunburypress.com

Camp Hill, Pennsylvania   USA

For Bob

Prologue

Icarus Falling

About suffering they were never wrong,
The old Masters: how well they understood
Its human position: how it takes place
While someone else is eating or opening a
window or just walking dully along...

W. H. Auden, "Musée des Beaux Arts"

If you fly into New Orleans and land at Louis Armstrong International Airport's Concourse C, as you walk from the gate into the terminal, look up. You will see hanging over the vast lobby a giant figure of Icarus, his golden wings unfurled, suspended high in the air above you. Icarus, son of Daedalus. The father fashioned wings of wax and feathers to let his son fly then watched as Icarus perished in the sea when he flew too near the sun, melting the wings. An odd choice of decoration for an airport, you might think.

Yet you've come to New Orleans, a city that pays yearly homage to Bacchus, Endymion, Orpheus, Proteus, and scores of other figures of Greco-Roman myth by staging in their names elaborate Mardi Gras balls and parades. Many of those parades celebrate the spirit of irony that is one of New Orleans' special cultural traits. Who better than Icarus to welcome the lately airborne to "the city that care forgot"?

It was that spirit of irony and joy, that "live and let live" attitude anchored in a reverence for history and tradition that attracted my husband Bob and me to New Orleans. We loved our work as professors in the same English department of a university in the Pennsylvania State system, but those roles meant the constraints of schedules and responsibilities and the sober demands of academia. Over the years, each time we broke away to visit New Orleans, we embraced more and more its

1

Mediterranean approach to time and living, its celebration of music and myth and good food and good stories, its rich mix of people and their *joie de vivre*, its seductive invitation to shed constraints and join the dance. Bob and I lived in and traveled to various places over our decades-long marriage, but each time we landed at Louis Armstrong International Airport, the blast of heat and tropical breezes that greeted us felt more and more like *home*. My husband's smile got wider as his feet hit the streets of the French Quarter, where any time of day the sounds of a brass band might blare from any direction, where the sweet scent of jasmine drifting from behind an iron gate seemed a promise of new adventures. The city had problems, to be sure: pervasive poverty, failing schools, simmering racial tensions, an insular government periodically accused of patronage, corruption, and incompetence. Yet the streetcars kept gliding up St. Charles Avenue, music filled the air, and the warmth of New Orleans' people and their exuberant culture cast an irresistible spell. Bob and I were happy almost anywhere as long as we were together—and we were nearly always together—but we were especially happy in New Orleans. Gradually we formed a plan: we would make a home in New Orleans, and when it was time to leave our teaching jobs, we'd begin the next phase of our life in the Crescent City.

The plan worked for awhile. Over a decade of visits during summers and school breaks, we found and renovated a small, 1840s-era Creole cottage in the city's oldest neighborhood. In the fall of 2003, we began our first full year of life in New Orleans, thrilled at finally being able to experience the city as residents, to enjoy the rich offerings of its tolerant lifestyle and quirky culture. In early 2004 when winter winds swept most of the country, we sat under the banana tree in our courtyard and marveled at our good fortune. "To the good life in the Big Easy," said Bob, raising his glass of pinot noir.

Fate had other plans for us. That April, Bob, a survivor of two cancers, got a third diagnosis. Together, we were swept up in the whirlwind of his illness and treatments, blown from doctor to doctor, lab to lab, procedure to procedure. Then came a true whirlwind.

When Hurricane Katrina blasted through New Orleans and the U. S. Army Corps of Engineers' flood walls and levees failed, when water from Lake Pontchartrain and surges from the Gulf of Mexico drowned New Orleans, Bob and I were caught in the disaster. Trapped in a flooded hospital, we waited as so many of those whose job it was to care—the Federal Emergency Management Agency, the Office of Homeland Security, government at all levels: federal, state, and local, but especially federal—turned away in the face of great need, and failed horribly. In the aftermath, I had time to contemplate that figure of Icarus suspended over the airport lobby, and I thought of Auden's "Musée des Beaux Arts" with its haunting images drawn from a Breughel painting: the plowman who hears the splash as Icarus falls into the sea, yet "turns away quite leisurely from the disaster," and the ship that sees the "boy falling out of the sky" and into the water but had "somewhere to get to and sailed calmly on."

The rest of the country, indeed the rest of the world, going about its business, watched transfixed as floodwaters swamped New Orleans. More than a thousand citizens perished in the waters. Others, marooned for days, endured fear and terrible suffering before being rescued, finally, by the U. S. Coast Guard, Wildlife and Fisheries boatmen, firefighters, police, medics, and scores of ordinary citizen heroes who proved they did care. Their individual stories are testaments to grief and pain and sometimes profound loss, but also to courage and the strength of the human spirit.

After a life together that was in many ways charmed, my husband and I were among those trapped in flooded New Orleans, then separated by the maelstrom.

This is our story.

Chapter One

Let Us Go Then, You and I

Saturday, August 27 ~ Sunday, August 28, 2005

If my husband Bob had to endure another hospital stay, he wasn't going alone. Over thirty-six years we'd rarely been apart, and I wasn't leaving him now.

The stern-faced doctor's eyes were serious behind round, rimless glasses. "I really think we should admit you to the hospital, Mr. Perry," she said. "You can continue the fluids and we can treat your nausea and diarrhea."

Bob and I were in the Emergency Room at Memorial Medical Center, a sprawling complex at the intersection of Napoleon and South Claiborne Avenues, where the section of New Orleans known as Uptown meets the Broadmoor neighborhood. It was Saturday, August 27. Earlier in the afternoon, I had found Bob bracing himself at our bathroom sink, too weak to walk, and made a desperate call to his oncologist, who said Bob's chemotherapy had caused dehydration. He'd ordered fluids, and now Bob was attached to an IV pumping bags of saline and minerals into his veins.

The ER doctor's words were unexpected, and I demurred. "But Dr. Veith told us we should just get fluids here and go back home," I said. "Does Bob really need to stay?"

"Where else will you go?" asked the doctor. "There's a hurricane coming. It's too late to leave, and you're better off here than in your house. We have people begging to be admitted. Your husband meets our admission criteria, and you'll be safer here. As soon as the storm passes on Monday, you can go home."

All week long, we had been watching as the system named Katrina tracked its way across the Gulf of Mexico.

4

Like most people in Louisiana, we had thought this storm was headed for Florida. But yesterday Katrina, now a powerful and wide-ranging hurricane, had veered westward. This morning, the mayor told the people of New Orleans to start evacuating. We took the warnings seriously, but our options were limited. In early August, Bob had started a new round of chemotherapy, this time with harsher drugs that were taking a toll on his already weakened body. I feared he couldn't endure a long car trip, especially the possibility of being stuck in traffic with only me to help him. Still, I hated the thought of him in the hospital again.

"I can stay here with him?" I asked.

"Yes, we have a private room for him, and you can stay there too. A lot of people are sheltering here. The hospital has emergency generators. You'll be comfortable and safe from the storm."

My head buzzed. I had wanted a quick fix. Yet supporting Bob's six-foot two-inch frame had been a struggle as we'd staggered from our house to the car. He was weaker than I'd ever seen him. A young ER nurse, looking concerned, had recorded his blood pressure at 68/48 and immediately started the IV. I rested the back of my hand on his cheek and looked in his eyes. "What do you think, Bob? Should we stay?"

"I guess so," he said. "I feel really rotten." He looked pale and miserable, lying with his feet hanging over the end of the ER bed. None of the hospitals we'd been in had beds long enough for Bob—he'd made half-joking complaints at first, but finally he became resigned to his feet hanging over each time his illness sent him to one of those too-short beds. I patted his shoulder and adjusted his pillow, trying to ease his discomfort.

The last time we'd been in a hospital, earlier in the summer, Bob had been impatient to get out and get home. That he agreed so readily now to stay made me realize how sick he must feel.

So I nodded to the stern-faced doctor and said, "Okay. Check us in." I knew Bob needed to get his strength back. He was due for another dose of chemo in ten days, and the schedule was rigid. A short hospital stay would solve his dehydration and he'd feel better. It did sound as if Memorial Hospital was a better place than our French Quarter cottage for us to shelter from the hurricane, and we'd be together. During all of Bob's hospitalizations, I'd stayed in his room, sleeping on cots or in chairs. In Houston during the first round of chemotherapy at the M.D. Anderson Cancer Center, I'd even spent a night sleeping on a blanket on the floor of his cubicle in the hospital's ER when we had an overnight crisis and had to wait until morning for a radiology procedure. In all the years of our marriage, Bob and I had spent only a few dozen nights apart, and I wouldn't leave him now. I couldn't have known that in a matter of days, Memorial Medical Center would force us to separate in a crisis none of us could have imagined.

The nurse, a dark-haired beauty with Erin on the name tag pinned to her blue scrubs, looked relieved when we agreed to stay. She filled out paperwork while we waited. "I'll have a room assignment in a minute," she said. "You'll definitely get a private room since you're on chemo, Mr. Perry. You're going to feel better soon with those fluids."

The hallway was full of bustle and noise, patients arriving on their own or by ambulance. A round-faced nun was brought into the cubicle next to us, accompanied by another nun. It was impossible not to eavesdrop through the flimsy partition, and we heard that the older nun had suffered chest pains during their convent's evacuation. A man in the hall had brought his aged mother to the hospital for shelter. He pleaded that she was too ill to leave town, but we heard the doctor explain that she wasn't sick enough to require hospital care and couldn't be admitted. The "admission criteria" the doctor had mentioned to us apparently determined which patients they could accept. I suppose we should have felt lucky that we were among the select.

Soon Bob was wheeled on a gurney through Memorial's halls, into the elevator, and up to the third floor of the hospital, me trailing behind. As I walked, I glanced into rooms and saw patients staring up at TVs, and voices of weathercasters echoed in the hallway. Aides moved Bob into his room in the Clara Wing, where he lay surrounded by institutional yellow walls, his bed parallel to a large window that ran the length of the room. His IV pole sat at one side of the bed, a small table and chair at the other. An aide soon wheeled in a rickety roll-away cot with a squishy mattress for me, and I set up my bed at the foot of the room, in a corner under the window. The scene was familiar: we'd spent several nights in this same wing of the hospital over the past year, when Bob's chemotherapy required overnight dosing and monitoring. In the little room, we had a sink, a private bathroom equipped with a shower and toilet, and a small TV suspended from the ceiling—our refuge from the storm.

"Well, we've got a nice view," I said, gazing out the window overlooking Clara Street, a side street off Napoleon Avenue. I'd parked our silver Accord at the curb below us, and now other cars were parking the length of the street, and people were unloading suitcases, coolers, small children. Many had animals on leashes or in cages. A steady stream of people seemed to be coming to the hospital. When a nurse came into our room, I asked her about all the people arriving.

She explained the tradition at Memorial when a hurricane threatened. "Some staff are on regular duty and others volunteer to come to work during storms. We're allowed to bring family and pets with us, so they can shelter here too. It's been done that way as long as I can remember."

"Where do the pets stay?" I asked.

"There's a room set aside, but it's filling up, and some are going to the parking garage."

In addition to the eight-story hospital building, the sprawling Memorial complex included a surgery/intensive care building and various office buildings, all spread over three blocks and connected to the hospital by suspended, glassed-in walkways. There were two multistory garages, one on the north side adjacent to an office building, the other on the opposite side of the hospital, the river side, opening onto Magnolia Street. From the section of New Orleans first settled, the Vieux Carré or "Old Square," now known as the French Quarter, the city's population had spread west, parallel to the Mississippi River along St. Charles Avenue, to the Garden District and beyond, into Uptown. Memorial Medical Center sat on the edge of Uptown, adjacent to the lower-lying neighborhoods running north toward Lake Pontchartrain and two and a half miles from the French Quarter, where we lived.

"What about patients?" I asked. "Is the hospital full?"

"Getting full," said the nurse. "We probably have about 300 patients. It's going to be a crazy few days." She had introduced herself as Carolyn. We shared the same first name, and we were about the same five-foot five-inch height, but in other ways she was quite different from me. Nurse Carolyn was blond and bustling, with a loud voice, a hearty laugh, and a brusque manner. She checked Bob's IV, told us to call her if we needed anything, and hurried out.

As Bob dozed, I made phone calls to let people know where we were. First, I called our friend Steve, who was about to leave town. His dog Bosco had been hit by a car fleeing the storm, and Steve and his partner were evacuating to Dallas, where the injured dog could have surgery. They'd suggested we drive behind them, at least as far as Lafayette, a small city a hundred miles west of New Orleans, so they'd be near if Bob needed help.

When Steve answered, I told him to leave without us. "We're in Memorial. Bob's been admitted and I'm staying with him." There was a pause.

"Memorial? Oh—you mean Baptist," said Steve. Founded in 1926, the hospital was known as Southern Baptist until it was purchased in 1996 by Tenet Healthcare and given a new name. Most locals still thought of it as Baptist. "Good. They'll take care of him. Call my cell phone after the storm and let me know how you both are. Take care."

Next, I made calls to our scattered family in North Carolina, Texas, and California. All said they were glad we were in the hospital, with its stock of supplies and emergency generator. "A hospital is one of the safest places to be in an emergency," said my sister Liz, who lives in

Oakland, scene of an earthquake and hill fires not long ago, so she'd had some experience with disasters.

As the evening wore on, we kept our eyes on the TV. Weather people from all over the country seemed to be gathering on the windy Gulf shores, waves crashing behind them, all trying to predict where the hurricane would make landfall. On all the forecasters' maps, the huge system that was Katrina, with its wide swath of clouds, whirling red hurricane symbol, and ominous yellow "cone of uncertainty" stretching for miles along the coast, still pointed straight toward New Orleans.

"Well," said Bob, "looks like we're going to be in the middle of it—another hurricane."

"Do you believe it?" I said. "One hurricane in a lifetime should be enough."

We'd been celebrating three years of marriage on June 21, 1972, when Hurricane Agnes threatened—of all places—central Pennsylvania. Bob had memories of riding out Hurricane Carla with his family on Galveston Island in 1961. I'd grown up in tornado-prone Oklahoma and knew of hurricanes only by reputation. When we married in 1969, we spent our first summer in Galveston and experienced the powerful western winds of Hurricane Camille as it tracked east, skirting New Orleans and wreaking terrible destruction in Mississippi. When we moved that fall from Galveston to Pennsylvania, we thought we were leaving behind the Gulf Coast and those fearsome storms with names.

Then in 1972 Agnes blew up the eastern seaboard and stalled, dumping rain for days on the Keystone State. Rivers were swollen, and in the early morning hours of June 22, the Susquehanna River, across the street from our townhouse on Water Street, rose over its banks. Bob and I hadn't evacuated that time, either. A neighbor had assured us that despite its name, our street wouldn't flood. Near midnight, we'd walked out to look at the bank-full river and then gone blithely to bed. After all, we were in the foothills of the Allegheny Mountains—how could a hurricane threaten us there?

We awoke to gurgling sounds of muddy water sloshing into our first floor. Trapped in our bedroom for hours as the water rose nearly five feet up the stairs, we knotted bed sheets together, climbed out our second-story window into a rescue boat, and were ferried through flooded streets, leaving a wake slapping against houses as we passed. Afterward, for months we cleaned mud and mold and tossed ruined possessions. We were young, but we swore *never again* and moved to higher ground.

For the next three decades, we lived high and dry on a hill above the Susquehanna, teaching English at Lock Haven University of Pennsylvania. Other rivers, lakes and oceans were destinations for travel, experienced briefly, in times of calm. Yet when the time came to retire from our jobs, the lure of the Gulf Coast pulled us south, and we headed once more to the part of the country where hurricane season stretches from June to November. We got hazard and flood insurance on our cottage in the French Quarter and vowed to stay watchful. When Hurricane Andrew blew into the Gulf just weeks before we closed the sale on the house, we watched nervously, but Andrew turned most of its fury toward Florida. Since then, only a few storms had threatened New Orleans. We told ourselves whenever one of those named storms approached, we'd be the first to evacuate.

That was the plan. Now Bob was locked in a fierce struggle with a cancer that he'd beat into remission once but now was back. Getting him well was all that mattered. So, in room 3158 at Memorial/Baptist, my husband and I became two of the thousands of people still in the city as Hurricane Katrina blew toward New Orleans.

When we awoke Sunday morning, our thoughts went immediately to the storm. "Let's check the TV," said Bob. "Maybe the thing changed direction in the night."

Instead, all channels were reporting the latest Weather Service warnings that Katrina was holding its track toward New Orleans, using phrases such as "unprecedented strength," "devastating damage expected," and "rivaling the intensity of Hurricane Camille of 1969." The voices of the local weather experts contained an underlying tone of panic that we'd not heard before. The word *mandatory* had now been added to the evacuation

order, and stations played recordings of Mayor C. Ray
Nagin's and Governor Kathleen Blanco's voices, urging
citizens to get out of New Orleans and the surrounding
parishes (the term used in Louisiana for what other states
call counties). The mayor's warning was vivid: he told
residents who were thinking of riding out the storm that
they'd better make sure they had not only food and water,
but also an ax, because they might have to chop their way
out of their attics. If he was trying to scare people, it was
working. The city's "contraflow" plan had started, making
all lanes of major roads one way leading out of the city,
and the TV showed long lines of cars crawling steadily out,
bumper to bumper. Those who had no transportation were
told to go to the Superdome, the designated "shelter of last
resort." About one third of the populace, or more than
140,000 people, did not own cars and had no way to leave
—it soon became clear that the city's evacuation plan for
these citizens was woefully inadequate, as were the plans
and provisions for sheltering them.

Early in the morning, Nurse Carolyn appeared and
told us Bob had been assigned to her care. She gave him
his morning pills, then hooked a new bag of fluids to the IV
pole. "Your chart says you're from Pennsylvania, Mr.
Perry," she said. "How'd you all end up here?"

"Too much snow," said Bob. "We retired where it's
warm. Didn't need this much warm."

Moving to a small town in rural Pennsylvania thirty-
six years ago had been culture shock for two people used
to cities, but we grew to love the wind-swept ridges of the
Allegheny Mountains and the verdant Susquehanna valley.
Yet we never got used to the winters.

"Retired? What work did you do?" asked Carolyn.

"Teacher," said Bob. "Forty years in the classroom.
We were both English teachers."

"Uh oh," said Carolyn. She glanced at me and I
knew what was coming—the response we got from so many
people when they heard those words. "I'll have to watch my
grammar in this room."

"Grammar's the least of our worries," said Bob.

"Bob was a Shakespeare professor," I said.

Carolyn looked intrigued. "I've always been interested in those plays. A friend of mine does costumes for the summer Shakespeare Festival at Tulane." She checked the tube attached to a needle stuck into Bob's arm. Then she cocked her head and looked at him. "I can see you teaching Shakespeare. You've got that look."

"What, flat on my back and tube-tied?" he said.

She laughed. "You're funny, too. Breakfast is on the way. Call me if you need me." She breezed out of the room.

Bob had loved his role as teacher of Renaissance, seventeenth-century, and world literature, and he discovered a special talent for teaching freshman writers. I soon joined the English faculty to teach writing and open a writing center, and we became a team at work as well as home. Sharing our teaching highs and lows, helping each other navigate the thorny byways of academia, and knowing and guiding the same students made us both happy. Best of all, we kept each other laughing. We indulged our southwest-induced love of football by following the team and volunteering as their academic advisors. In the breaks, we took long trips—to the UK, to Greece, to Italy, to various places in North America. We looked forward to a lot more travel in the future, but first we had to get past this cancer. We hadn't figured on a hurricane as well.

In the hospital, staff went about their routines, though an air of anticipation was building. Hallways and waiting areas had filled with people, with family groups creating mini-camps, their sleeping bags, blankets, and pillows arrayed on furniture and floors. Approximately two thousand people, including patients, staff, and family members, plus hundreds of pets, were in Memorial Hospital, waiting for Katrina.

After a stroll through the hallways, I described the scene to Bob: "You wouldn't believe the mob in this hospital. Every lobby and waiting room is packed with people."

"All fool," said Bob.

That made me chuckle. "Right. Definitely 'All fool'." The phrase was a relic of our first trip to Greece, the second summer after we married. Bob had traveled there before and was eager to show me the land of Homer and his wine-dark sea, so we hopped from island to island by ferry. After we'd decided on dates and destinations, Bob had spent weeks planning our trip, writing letters to confirm reservations. But on the island of Mykonos, we encountered a major snafu: the hotel had booked us for only one night instead of the five we'd planned. The desk clerk told us additional nights weren't possible and suggested we try the tourist bureau to find another hotel. Bob was furious.

"We'll stay here tonight, then we'll take the ferry back to Athens," he said, his voice terse.

"Let's at least try the tourist bureau," I said.

"It's high summer. This hotel is full. Other hotels are going to be full, too. I'm not staying in some hovel."

I recognized the mood of implacability coming over him and changed the subject. "Well, at least we have today and tonight. Let's go explore Mykonos."

Bob's glum mood lasted all afternoon as we wandered the sun-dazzled island, with its white windmills and blue-shuttered houses. Over dinner in a taverna's garden he brightened somewhat, but as we walked back to the hotel, all he could talk about was the ferry schedule. I was silent. I still hoped we'd find a way to stay.

The next morning a taxi deposited us and our bags in the town center in front of the ferry office. The adjacent tourist bureau was closed.

"Before you buy the tickets," I said, "let's at least try some hotels. Maybe we'll get lucky."

"I am not dragging these bags all over Mykonos, begging for a hotel room," said Bob.

There's no better way to learn about someone's personality than to travel with him. Bob's careful plans had been thwarted. He was ready to change course, and he wasn't going to waste time on a wild goose chase.

"Okay," I said. "You wait here with the bags. We have time. Give me thirty minutes just to look." My stubborn streak was coming out. We'd planned to stay on Mykonos and visit the nearby island of Delos. I wasn't giving up so easily.

Bob flashed me a long-suffering look, took a breath, and agreed. "Thirty minutes." He moved the suitcases to a nearby bench and sat, looking disgruntled. Bob had a hard time being patient, but he seldom tried to deter me from something I really wanted.

I checked my watch and started toward the town center, praying I wouldn't get lost in the maze of the island's bustling streets. Clerks at the first two hotels I tried gave me smiles of regret and shook their heads. "Sorry, no. All full." They pronounced the English words as "*All fool.*" Maybe Bob had been right: this was a wild goose chase.

Deciding to give it ten more minutes, I rounded a corner and encountered a large, two-story whitewashed building, with bright red geraniums in pots by the door and purple bougainvillea spilling off iron balconies. If I'd tried to conjure a vision of an ideal hotel in a Greek island village, this would be it.

A middle-aged woman with an angular face, onyx eyes and gray-streaked black hair smiled from behind a counter at my attempt at *Kaliméra*, the Greek for "Good morning." Of the Greek words I'd learned, it was easiest to remember because it resembled the calamari we often ordered for dinner. Then I had to revert to English.

She frowned at my request. "Four nights? No." I sighed. Then she said, "You can have a room for three nights." She explained that a regular guest would arrive on the fourth day and had booked his usual room. Until then, that room was available. It turned out to be spacious and airy, with a balcony overlooking the town, and a cost that was less than we would have paid at our original hotel. When I returned to Bob sitting glumly on his bench, surrounded by bags, I felt like the Goddess of Fortune.

Those three days were among the happiest we spent in Greece, and in the end the hotel let us move to a small basement room for the fourth night. Each morning we lingered over coffee in an outdoor café presided over by Pello, a dour pelican who perched stone-like on one of the tables, begging for bread. After breakfast, we wandered the village, visited the ruins at Delos, or lay on white sand beaches gazing over the glistening Aegean.

Mykonos foretold a pattern that lasted in our marriage. Bob was the planner, the meticulous organizer of details, the conductor choreographing the performance. When the unexpected happened, that was my cue to step in, and my stubborn persistence often got us past the obstacles. Laughter always helped. In the shared vocabulary that develops between long-married partners, from then on our catch phrase to signify a snafu in any plan, a snafu with the potential for serendipity, became the words *All fool*.

Katrina was a snafu, all right. Would the storm bring us any serendipity?

At lunchtime, a Memorial aide brought Bob's tray. He was feeling better as the IV fluids and medications did their work. The breezy Nurse Carolyn returned in late morning. Both of us had liked and trusted Carolyn at once. She was matter-of-fact, outspoken, and efficient, with the added bonus of a sense of humor: her pointed comments about trying to work amidst the crowds of people gathering in the hospital made us smile. Now she told us that she'd checked the supply room and discovered that the hospital didn't have the particular type of dressing that worked best for a wound Bob had, the result of an earlier procedure to deal with a kidney obstruction.

"I didn't bring any because I didn't know we'd be staying," I said. "I could go back to the house and get some."

"Well, you'll be here for today and tomorrow, so that's probably a good idea," said Carolyn. "But go now if you're going, so you can get back before the winds get too bad and the rain starts. You don't want to have to swim up St. Charles Avenue." That image seemed comical at the time.

Going now sounded like a good idea. I could get the supplies and also close up the house more tightly than we'd left it. So, early Sunday afternoon, I bent to give Bob a hug and told him I'd be back soon.

"Don't be too long," he said, clinging to my hand for a minute, a vertical worry line between his eyebrows. "You'll be careful, won't you?"

I squeezed his hand. "Don't worry, I'll be fine. I'll close up the house, get the stuff and be right back."

The sky was darkening as I drove the few miles down St. Charles Avenue, through the Garden District and across the Central Business District to our home in the French Quarter. Fearing what the wind and water might do, I moved some things off the floors and filled the bathtub with water, a trick I remembered from Hurricane Agnes back in Pennsylvania, when water service stopped for several days, and we had to use stored water to flush toilets. Now, I walked around our small house, trying to think how to prepare it. I closed windows and doors, battened their heavy cypress shutters, and secured loose objects in the courtyard. The wind was starting to whip around the back corner of the house, rattling the big ginger leaves. Fronds on the banana plant in the corner were blowing wildly and starting to fray. I spoke a few soothing words to the three goldfish in our small pond—they would, I hoped, survive placidly underwater as Katrina raged above them.

Back inside, I packed clothes for one or two more days in the hospital. Next, I stuffed a tote bag with our numerous medications and the supplies for Bob. I also decided to take along our laptop computer and two portable file boxes containing important papers—financial records, tax files, personal papers—as well as some computer disks and my camera, thinking they'd be safer in the hospital room with us. On impulse, I picked up the framed wedding photo sitting on a bookshelf. Bob's left arm is around my waist, his right hand holding a champagne glass. I'm leaning into his shoulder and we both have mile-wide smiles on our faces.

Bob had proposed over the phone as I sat in my car in mid-winter, parked at the edge of a cow pasture outside Goodwell, Oklahoma, buffeted by wind, clutching to my ear the black handset of a highway pay phone, hardly remembering to breathe. I said yes.

I was teaching English at Panhandle State College, under contract for the academic year. The windswept campus edged the tiny town of Goodwell, in the heart of what had been the 1930s Dust Bowl. Bob was just back from two years of study in London, living in Galveston, Texas, and working as a temporary writer for the U. S. Army Corps of Engineers while he searched for a teaching post. The weekend after he proposed, Bob came to Goodwell bearing an engagement ring and two dozen Gulf Coast oysters packed in dry ice, but for the next four months, except for a few more short meetings, we were separated by more than seven hundred flat, endless southwestern miles. Letters were our lifeline, and in them we swore that once we were married, there would be no more separations.

I knew Bob would be worrying now—I'd told him I wouldn't be gone long. I stuffed the wedding picture in a bag. What else should I take? Ah—the vinyl pouch containing our checkbook and a stash of cash. Where had I last seen it?

I walked to the back room, with its French doors opening to the courtyard. Outside, the wind was blowing harder, showering leaves from the sweet olive tree into the pond and making the banana and ginger leaves hiss and click as they knocked against each other.

I turned to the cupboard in the corner. It was Bob's favorite piece of furniture, and it was where he usually kept the black bank envelope. Fashioned of old cypress, gnarled and gouged in places, the cupboard held a hoard of treasures. In the center of the open shelf was the flamingo vase Bob spotted at the St. Jude Community Center auction and had to have—started at two dollars and upped the bidding until he won it for the grand sum of sixteen dollars. The work of a New Orleans potter, it featured two purple flamingos, their long necks fading to pink and curving as handles on either side of the green vase, garish and wonderful. Next to it was the framed photo, taken by a nephew, of Bob standing next to a giant bronze pig named Clementine, outside the Santa Fe hotel where we'd gone for a family wedding, the last trip before his diagnosis in April 2004. The pig, double Bob's weight, sits on huge haunches, her head waist-high. Bob's hand is on the pig's head, and they're both grinning. On the opposite side of the shelf, behind a small picture of the two of us at a local restaurant the previous Thanksgiving, was a photo of a purple swamp iris, reminder of the "walking" iris in our courtyard and one of the items on our list of *things to do after chemo is over*: visit Jean Lafitte Park in March to see the iris. March seemed a long way in the future this August day.

Above the shelf, behind glass doors, was the crystal pitcher we found at the factory in Waterford, Ireland, on that trip when the solar eclipse caught us on the road outside Cork, and the skies went suddenly dark, mid-day. We'd pulled the car over and stopped to watch in awe as greyness rolled over the eerie landscape, then light slowly returned. At the back of the shelf, standing exuberantly on edge, was the bright bamboo tray, stained the color of hot sauce. Its front showed a splash of oysters surrounding a tall bottle of Tabasco, souvenir from our tour of Avery Island in fall of 2004, where, cancer-free after the first chemo, we celebrated our return to normalcy. Very little had been normal since, and now here we were, stranded with a hurricane bearing down, about as far from normal as we could get. I stuck my hand behind the tray, but the bank pouch wasn't there.

Under the shelf, the lower section of the cabinet behind wooden doors contained my copy of *Southern Cooking* and the 10-quart pot Bob used for his special recipes. We'd designed the kitchen so we could cook together. Bob's recipes were usually dramatic productions. I'd chop—too randomly and not precisely enough for his taste, but he liked the help. As in almost every other way, we were compatible as cooks, enjoying the togetherness and teasing each other about our differences. Bob would assemble his "secret spices" and other ingredients, putting it all together with a flourish. Two weeks after he proposed to me, Bob had suddenly announced he'd ordered Julia Child's *Mastering the Art of French Cooking* as a gift for me, "So you can learn to cook."

My reaction was intense: "So *I* can learn to cook? Let's talk about these assumptions you seem to have, my friend." I wondered what I'd gotten myself into. Was I marrying Ward Cleaver? Was this engagement a huge mistake? But it wasn't. I did learn to cook, and to love doing it. Bob always applauded my efforts and enjoyed the results, and along the way he found intriguing recipes that inspired him to try his own hand at the stove. He discovered he enjoyed cooking, too. The best part of renovating the old New Orleans house was the chance to create our dream kitchen. How long would it be before I'd see him standing at the stove, stirring his red beans or Texas chili, or trying the new gumbo recipe he'd found? I peered behind the pot in the bottom of the cupboard, and there it was at last. I pulled out the fat, envelope-sized bank pouch, stuffing it into my shoulder bag. The rest of our belongings would have to stay. I made two trips to the car, then closed the shutters over our front door and locked the outside gate.

"Be safe, house," I said aloud.

Matassa's, the neighborhood grocery on the corner, was doing a brisk business on this Sunday afternoon, with a crowd of people stocking up on water and other basics. We had a supply of bottled water in the house, and we'd have plenty of food when we returned from the hospital: our refrigerator contained a cooked ham, the freezer held bags of frozen shrimp, and the pantry was stocked. I waited in line to buy a Sunday *Times-Picayune* to take back to Memorial. Among the benefits of living in the French Quarter, a small area seven blocks wide by thirteen blocks long, were the many such neighborhood shops and delicatessens, particularly in the lower, more residential part of the Quarter. Besides offering a wide array of groceries, Matassa's was "news central" for the neighborhood. The small store's shelves were packed and its narrow aisles usually crammed with boxes and cartons of everything from pet food to fine wine. Getting past someone in an aisle meant turning sideways and squeezing by, so close encounters and friendly chats, with neighbors as well as strangers, were routine. Today people were talking about whether they'd ride out the storm or leave. I greeted a red-headed neighbor from around the corner.

"Are you leaving, Paula?"

"Can't face being cooped up in a car with our huge dog," she said. Trident, their Great Dane, was a well-known neighborhood denizen. "Not sure it's the right decision—now that the wind's picking up I'm having second thoughts. But it's too late to go now, so guess we're staying. What about you?"

"Bob's at Baptist Hospital and I'm staying there with him, so we'll see you on Tuesday. Take care."

Many of the customers in line at the cash register were having the same conversation, most wishing each other luck wherever they were going, some vowing to stay no matter what. The Matassa family, the store's owners for three generations, were preparing to evacuate—something rare for them. Like many native New Orleanians, they measured each threat by comparing it to Hurricane Betsy, the last major hurricane to hit the city back in 1965. They tended to be blasé about mere warnings, but Katrina had their attention.

The sky was the color of dull pewter, with clouds roiling, and the thick August heat enveloped me as I walked the short distance to the car. I drove slowly out of the Quarter, toward bordering Canal Street. Along the narrow blocks, people were boarding up doors and windows of houses and storefronts with huge sheets of plywood. Duct tape was no protection from a hurricane—openings that didn't have shutters needed to be covered. Wrestling the big boards into place was sweaty work with the temperature in the nineties and high humidity, and some workers had shed shirts and wore sweatbands or towels on their heads. The French Quarter's lacy iron balconies were bare of furniture, and the huge ferns and flower baskets hanging from galleries and railings had either been removed or were swaying and creaking in the strengthening winds. There was nothing refreshing about the breeze—the air was hot, and smelled metallic.

I headed uptown toward the hospital, and traffic seemed much lighter than on a normal Sunday afternoon. Rain began to hit the windshield as I passed a Winn Dixie supermarket, shut and boarded up, and several drug stores, their doors also covered with plywood. Luckily, I had heeded advice earlier in the week and filled prescriptions, gassed up the car, and gotten a supply of cash, another lesson I remembered from Hurricane Agnes, when ready cash was the only way to get necessities.

In the Central Business District, streets were almost deserted, although I passed a few individuals and small groups making their way on foot toward the Superdome in the rain, most carrying plastic trash sacks stuffed with clothes over their shoulders, their arms around pillows and blankets. A few dragged or carried coolers. People had been told to come to the Superdome only if they had "special needs" or no way to evacuate, and they were to bring with them enough food and water for three days. City officials had announced that no services were planned for the Dome, apparently as a way to convince people to leave town. Yet no transportation was provided for those who wanted to evacuate but had no way to leave. One out of three city residents fit that description, and a large percentage of them ended up in the Superdome or, later, the Convention Center. Neither shelter was adequately stocked with food or water.

Returning the couple of miles to the hospital complex, I saw cars parked sideways on the grassy central medians along wide Napoleon and South Claiborne Avenues. New Orleanians called these medians "neutral grounds." Lower-lying streets in New Orleans sometimes had trouble draining in heavy rains, and residents of nearby neighborhoods often pulled their cars onto the high neutral grounds to keep them dry.

Turning off Napoleon, I tried to enter the Magnolia garage but was stopped by a security guard wearing a fluorescent-striped vest. "Sorry, Miss, garage reserved for hospital employees." His face was stern but his eyes were kind.

"My husband's a patient and I'm staying with him. Is there any way I can park up high? I don't want to leave our car on the street. I'm afraid it'll get hit with flying stuff."

"Can't let you now," he said. "Maybe later. Staff still coming in."

I went back to the garage several times through the afternoon, exercising what Bob often called my "obsessive gene," an unwillingness to give up when there was something I really wanted, sometimes persisting beyond all reason. This time it paid off, and near dusk, on my fourth try, the guard gave me a smile. "Some spaces up on seven," he said, and waved me through.

I thanked him and drove slowly up the ramps to the seventh level. Along the way, I passed vehicles parked in every space. Beginning on the second level, animal cages of all sizes were lined up against the back wall of the garage and interspersed among the parked cars, trucks, and vans. Even with my car windows closed, the barks and yaps of the dogs and the screech of at least one caged bird followed me as I drove. Another large enclave of animals was on three, and some on the fourth and fifth levels as well. The four walls of the garage were brick over concrete, but along the front and one side the walls were only waist high, with open space above, so at each level the animals had some air and light coming into the dank garage. Still, ceilings were low, and dust hung in the gloomy air. I imagined the animals were feeling the oppressive heat and humidity of the late August afternoon. Finally reaching seven, I stowed our car in an interior space, near the top of the garage. It should be safe from the wind here, I thought as I walked back to the elevator. The air smelled stale.

There were two ways to get from the Magnolia garage into the hospital. You could exit the elevator on the ground level and walk out the garage entry to the street, make a sharp left, and walk a short distance to a side door of the hospital building. The easier way was to take the elevator to the second level, where a door on the opposite side of the elevator opened directly into the hospital's second floor lobby. That was the way we'd come the last time, when aides had wheeled Bob out of the hospital and helped him to the car. He'd been a patient in Memorial for a week last spring, fighting a virulent infection that had necessitated a procedure to place a temporary tube into his back to drain a kidney. I'd been glad then that I always stayed in his room: I was the one who noticed in the middle of the night that the drain was blocked and alerted a nurse, who fixed it. That drain and powerful antibiotics had stopped the infection, and Bob smiled at me as he settled into the car, glad to be going home. "Let's blow this joint," he said, strapping himself carefully into the seat.

Supplies for the drain had been the reason for my trip home today, and now I punched the button and waited for the elevator to take me back to the second-level entrance to the hospital. Just the short walk from the car had caused perspiration to bead my forehead and neck. I'd be glad to get out of the sticky heat and into the hospital's air conditioning. Howls from the makeshift kennel below pierced the sultry air.

Back in our room, the phones still worked, so we talked to family once again, assuring everyone we were fine. Just in case, I told my sister where to find our wills. I didn't really think we were in mortal danger, but the atmosphere of dread that was building in the hospital and the city was enough to make me at least consider the possibility.

Bob was feeling a bit better, still weak and still getting fluids, but facing the ordeal with his habitual sense of humor. He had worked his usual charm on the nurses, making them laugh with his wry comments, and thanking them for each ministration in the courtly way he had. Like his former students and colleagues, nurses and doctors warmed to Bob's innate enthusiasm, the feeling he conveyed that he was genuinely glad to meet them and interested in who they were. Even laid low by disease, Bob had a way of listening closely, of making eye contact and talking directly, usually building in some lighthearted humor, and these nurses responded. I was grateful to have help caring for him, and thankful we weren't stuck in a motel somewhere, or on the road looking for one.

"The storm is definitely coming," I said to Bob. "The feeling reminds me of that morning during Agnes. And that was mainly water, not wind. This is scary. I'm glad we're in this hospital."

In answer, Bob gave me, in his sonorous voice, a quote from one of his favorite poems:

> Let us go then, you and I,
> when the evening is spread out against the sky,
> like a patient etherised upon a table;

23

He'd spoken those lines from T. S. Eliot's "The Love Song of J. Alfred Prufrock" often in the past. Never had they seemed so apt.

We passed an uneasy evening watching storm reports, laughing about the crazy weather people trying to stand upright in front of cameras in gale-force winds. But we also noted the rising alarm in their voices and wondered whether they—and we—would be safe. It seemed that Katrina was indeed going to be what New Orleanians called "the Big One."

Chapter Two

Blow, Winds

Monday, August 29

When I opened my eyes, I was staring at the window. The pre-dawn light was silver grey, the sound of the wind a high whine. Rain hit the windows and ran down in opaque sheets, punctuated by booms of thunder and flashes of lightning. When Nurse Carolyn came in with Bob's morning pills, she didn't turn on the lights.

"Power's off," she said, "but the back-up generator's on."

"So my pump's pumping," said Bob.

She grinned. "Oh, yes, Mr. Perry, don't you worry—that IV will keep going like the Energizer bunny."

We'd had a lot of experience with IV pumps. They had back-up batteries that would run for awhile, but their time was limited. I thought about all the many different machines that must be in use in the hospital—ventilators, oxygen tanks, dialysis machines, other equipment I couldn't even imagine. The generators were crucial. But they only worked for essential power, so regular lights and TVs were dead.

"What's happening with the storm?" I asked the nurse.

"They say it turned slightly to the east overnight, so New Orleans is not getting hit as directly as they thought," Carolyn said. "But it's really blowing out there." That was an understatement—the roar outside could be heard even through our insulated windows. Gusts blew thick bursts of rain against the glass. The sky outside was grey and filled with water.

An aide delivered Bob's breakfast tray, and after he finished eating, I took a quick shower—we still had warm water, which was unexpected but welcome—then started down to the basement cafeteria to find some coffee and breakfast for myself. A few of the nurses' computers were powered up in the hallway, attached to red emergency plugs, so at least we were still connected to the outside world. As I passed the nurses' station, a voice on a radio was talking about wind velocity and rainfall measurements. Katrina had come ashore at Buras, Louisiana, about 65 miles southeast of New Orleans, a strong Category Three hurricane with winds measured at 130 mph and a huge 27-ft storm surge.

The third-floor waiting area near the elevators looked like a slumber party, with sofas and the floor covered with blankets and sleeping bags, nodding heads still poking out of some. Families were grouped together, with small children lying next to parents, grandparents, or older siblings. Half-empty bags of chips and cookies and soft-drink cans were scattered around. A sign directed me up to the fourth floor, where people of all ages were waiting in a long line for food. Sausage, eggs, and grits were being doled out from a makeshift serving line. Instead, I turned and headed down to the basement. The cafeteria was nearly deserted, but I found some hot coffee, cold milk, and a box of cereal, all I wanted. As I walked back through the crowds in the lobby, voices chattered and the atmosphere was almost jovial—the hurricane was raging outside, but here in the hospital we were safe. The 79-year-old building was crowded and a bit uncomfortable, but it was protecting us, and people were making the best of it.

Back in our room, the day wore on. Outside, the winds got increasingly wild. The sky was charcoal grey, streaked with lightning. The rain appeared horizontal, and the sound of the wind was a sustained roar, rising and falling but always there. It bent trees over in the neighborhoods around the hospital. Fences flapped and awnings shook. The light was grey and eerie. Rainwater poured onto the cars parked in the street below us, and several cars and campers parked in a slightly raised lot on the other side of Clara Street were almost invisible in the driving rain.

I had always liked thunderstorms, especially the New Orleans kind, which were likely to arise suddenly on random summer afternoons, cutting through the tropical heat with rumblings of thunder, cool breezes, and saturating rain—as Blanche says in *A Streetcar Named Desire*, the "long rainy afternoons in New Orleans, when an hour isn't an hour but a little piece of eternity dropped in your hands...." But this rain was different. The wail and force of Katrina's winds were primeval and frightening.

Pop. Pop. Pop.

The sounds came suddenly, like gunshots, hard to hear over the sound of the winds, but somehow different. Soon no-nonsense Carolyn came bustling into our room.

"Windows in that walkway over Clara Street are blowing out," she said, "and a big window by the waiting room on this floor has cracked and broken. Rain's blowing in, floor to ceiling. It's a mess. We have to move people out of there. Now they're gonna be even more underfoot."

Before long, young men carried sofas and chairs and set them up in the hallways outside our room and along the hall on both ends of the nurses' station. Children were led by the hand, and a few adults also congregated in these new waiting areas.

Inside our room, Bob and I gazed out at the violent winds, which seemed to roar on and on, relentlessly. After awhile, a dark-haired nurse named Joanne appeared. We recognized her from a previous visit—she was a charge nurse on the oncology unit, and she had impressed us as calm and cool, the type who kept everything under control. Now she rushed into the room and put both her hands up flat on our windows. "I'm checking to see if the glass is vibrating," she said. "If you hear an odd noise, call us and we'll move you into the hall." She rushed out.

"Well, that's alarming," Bob said.

"Lord, I hope all that glass doesn't break," I replied. "And I really hope we don't have to move to the hall—it's crazy out there." Cocooned in our room, I sat at his bedside, holding his hand, both of us astonished at the storm's fury. Rain blew against the window and spread, forming a watery membrane.

"I wonder if the storm will damage the aquarium," I said. "Do you think they evacuated all the fish?"

"I doubt it," said Bob. "That would've taken weeks. I know they have big generators. The tanks are thick acrylic and the building's solid. It'll probably be all right."

More than a year ago, the aquarium graduation ceremony had taken place in front of stingrays and sharks. "Bob Perry," said the woman at the podium in the dim auditorium.

Behind her, a two-story wall of turquoise water shimmered. Light from above streaked the water, casting a giant undulating web on the back side of the tank. Short bursts of tiny bubbles drifted to the top. Soft background music from a synthesizer suggested underwater sound waves and matched the rhythm of the gliding fish. A pale sand tiger shark slid by, its beady eyes probing the water. Beside me, Bob rose from his seat on the bleachers. As he walked the five yards to the podium, a school of silver blue runners swam in front of us from the left, threading the barnacle-covered base of a model oil rig. A grey stingray flopped near the sandy bottom, and a five-foot-long lavender tarpon, scales shining like tin foil, came in from the right.

"Congratulations, and welcome to the volunteer staff of the Audubon Aquarium," the woman said as she handed Bob a certificate, then pinned a brass nameplate to his shirt. The nameplate read "Volunteer Bob," to be worn on his official uniform, a creamy polo shirt with the Audubon Nature Institute logo that featured a tiger, butterfly, and shark.

I had often heard Bob tell his former students, "I fell in love with universities when I was eighteen, and I never left." After a forty-year teaching career, he finally did leave the university, but he wasn't finished learning. In mid-winter of 2004, he decided to try something new: he'd train to be a volunteer guide at New Orleans' Aquarium of the Americas. The training ended with a ceremony at the shark tank, officially called the Gulf of Mexico Exhibit.

Each week, Bob had come home from the training sessions more knowledgeable and more enthusiastic about the prospect of guiding visitors to the aquarium's exhibits.

He took me with him on after-hours visits to search for the answers on the take-home final test, a kind of scavenger hunt that required close observation of angelfish, seahorses, penguins, jellyfish, sharks, sea otters, frogs and the other inhabitants of the various galleries, so I learned a lot, too.

Every Thursday, Bob attached his name tag to his official shirt, left our cottage in the lower Quarter, walked the few blocks to St. Louis Cathedral, and crossed Jackson Square. Often he stopped at a small cafe, picked up a bag of donuts to go, and carried them on the walk along the river to the aquarium, where he would share them with the other volunteers as they met to drink coffee and get their shift assignments. The aquarium volunteers usually rotated among the various areas. One shift might be at the Mississippi River Gallery and the next in the Amazon Rainforest—Bob enjoyed the feisty macaws there. The birds would preen for visitors, fluffing their bright red and blue feathers and squawking loudly. "Show-offs," Bob called them. The guides' mission was to interpret the exhibits for visitors, to answer questions, and generally to help people enjoy and learn from their aquarium experience. At the end of the day, Bob would come home smiling.

One Thursday, he walked in especially buoyant. "Where'd you work today?" I asked, coming in from the courtyard where I'd been pruning ginger.

"Spent most of the time at the Shark Touchpool," said Bob. "I think it's my favorite. There's always a long line of kids, from tiny on up. Some of them stick their hand right in the water, but a lot have to be convinced it's okay to touch the baby sharks. Today there was a prissy little girl, about six, I'd guess. She kept her arms folded tight, hands on elbows, and looked me in the eye." Bob dramatized as he told me the story.

"'Is that a real shark?' she said." He spoke with a hint of that "prissy" six-year-old voice.

"I told her, 'Yes, it's a real baby shark, called a nurse shark. Use two fingers, gently, and you can touch it.'

"'Is it going to bite me?' She gave me a fierce stare.

"'Bite you?' I said to her. 'What *must* you think of us? This aquarium wouldn't let a shark bite you. Go

29

ahead, touch it. You'll be surprised how soft it is.' She looked up at her mother, then at me, then at the shark. Finally she made up her mind. She stuck her hand in the water and ran two fingers the whole length of the shark's back. Then she flashed me a dazzling smile," said Bob. "It was great."

Now, sitting by Bob's bed, I thought about Katrina's powerful winds battering that building at the river's edge. "I hope the penguins and sea otters don't get freaked by the storm." Rain blew against our window as lightning flashed.

I looked at Bob. "Remember the little girl at the Shark Touchpool?" Outside, the wind wailed.

"Miss Priss," he said.

I smiled. "Who'd have thought you'd end up convincing little kids to take a chance and touch a shark?"

"When you think about it," Bob said, "it's not too different from teaching Shakespeare to twenty-year-olds."

I'd been twenty when I enrolled as a college junior in a Modern Drama course at the University of Dallas. The instructor was Robert O. Perry. He was fresh out of SMU graduate school, only twenty-eight but already an engaging, inspiring teacher. Bob's tall build, Nordic pale hair, and ever-present horn-rimmed glasses gave him a professorial look, but behind the glasses his eyes had a merry, impish glint, and his sense of humor could range from eruditely incisive to delightfully silly. Even then, early in his career, he knew how to make the plays we were reading come alive. His sense of drama infused his classroom, where discussions were lively and Bob's witty comments on the texts and on life's passing panorama were darkly ironic, sometimes sarcastic, usually insightful, and always entertaining. I looked forward to every session. But I was just one student of many, until a day in early spring when I challenged his interpretation of an Ibsen play we were reading. That was when he noticed me.

I stayed after class to question something he said about a character's motives in *Peer Gynt*. The details are fuzzy now—I disagreed with something Bob had said about Ase, Peer's mother, and proposed a different interpretation.

We walked up the hill to Bob's office in another building, where the argument continued for another fifteen minutes.

"I don't think you're right about her," he said, "but you've seen something in the character that I hadn't considered. Let's both re-read the scene and we'll talk again."

I left his office elated that such a learned professor had listened to me and valued my opinion. I worked doubly hard for the rest of the semester, though I didn't change his mind about Ase.

Later, Bob told me, "I wasn't always thinking about Ibsen when I met your eye in that class." But it was the still-proper early sixties, and he never let on. I finished college and went on to graduate school at Washington University in St. Louis and then to teaching jobs, and he soon left Dallas to study in England. We were both rebounding from loss when we met again, by chance through a mutual friend, nearly five years later. Within weeks, the earth had shifted, the heavens aligned, and suddenly the future was clear: we were meant to be together. After the phoned proposal by the cow pasture and the long-distance courtship, we married in June of 1969.

"Wherever that little girl is, she's probably still talking about the shark," I said now, glancing from the window to Bob. "You're pretty good with the ladies, whatever their age."

"It helps if they're smart—and argumentative."

The relentless wind made Monday a long, long day. Bob's lunch and dinner trays came on schedule. He didn't eat much, so I ate his leftovers. Staff maneuvered around the children, who amused themselves with games, their excited chatter and giggles filling the hallways outside our room. Several ran around with odd-looking balloons, white with strange protuberances. Someone had given them latex gloves, and they'd blown them up and tied them at the wrist. The palm parts were round puffs with inflated fingers sticking up. They looked like flying white cow udders, and the kids batted them back and forth, laughing. One little girl had a portable CD player, with a cartoonish, high-pitched voice singing the title song from *Beauty and the Beast*. She played it over and over, all afternoon:

Just a little change, small to say the least...
Both a little scared, neither one prepared,
Beauty and the Beast.

That song lodged in my brain. I'll never hear it again without hearing Katrina's winds howling in the background.

All day, powerful blasts of rain blew against the hospital and surrounding buildings. Despite the threat that the glass might break, I was drawn to the window, mesmerized by the fury outside. The streets surrounding the Memorial complex were lined with old double or single-family homes, most in the long, narrow "shotgun" style found throughout New Orleans. Winds were battering their weathered clapboards, and rainwater pooled in the yards, swamping the elephant ears and jasmine. The narrow streets around us were deserted: no people walking, no traffic moving, only the raging wind. At one end of Clara Street, the playground for the hospital's day care program was muddy and empty. Rain pounded the monkey bars, and the chain-link swings shimmied and flopped. Trees bent and broke in the wind. Water pooled and eddied in the street, the gusts kicking up whitecaps. Shingles flew off roofs in nearby neighborhoods, and awnings and whole porches tore from their moorings. Fences collapsed, were lifted up, and danced down the street. The force of the wind blew a white convertible slowly down the slope of the parking lot across from us, into the street. Water from the driving rain swirled up from the gutters and half-covered its wheels.

"This is unlike anything I've ever seen," I said to Bob. "The hospital seems solid, but the neighborhood around us is disintegrating."

Blow winds, and crack your cheeks. Rage! Blow! You cataracts and hurricanoes....

After forty years of teaching Shakespeare, Bob could pull out a quote for every occasion, delivered in his deep, forceful voice. That voice—a baritone with a hint of bass—was one of Bob's most distinctive features. He always spoke with easy inflection and could project his voice effortlessly. His students told me they loved to hear him read aloud because his voice had such expression and depth. Bob's whole classroom presence had been imposing: with his tall height, his large, light-haired head, trim build and deep voice, he was in constant motion, never standing behind a lectern but instead roaming around the room, talking or reading as he moved, or engaging in quick-witted give and take with students, smoothly commanding their attention.

"Nice voice, but you don't make a very convincing Lear, with your bald head," I teased him now. "Too bad you lost your Toscanini 'do'."

The blond hair Bob had when we met, remnant of his Swedish heritage, had gradually paled over the years, but it stayed thick. Before chemo he'd had a full head of wavy white hair that gave him a distinguished look, the shock falling over his forehead adding a hint of the boyish prankster he also was. My own brunette hair had gradually lightened and, once I stopped trying to defy nature, turned an almost identical shade of white, as if the years together were melding us into a white-haired pair. Watching Bob's fall out had been hard, but he was stoic. The morning it began to go, over the splash of the shower came his full-throated song. "It is the dawning of the Age of Aquarius," he sang with gusto, the theme from *Hair*. When, after the first chemo was over, his hair grew back, it came in tight white curls. He called them "chemo curls" and announced they made him look like Toscanini. The latest chemo had left him hairless again. As a joke, I'd bought him a fake diamond magnetized stud for one ear, giving him a jaunty look.

"Too bad we left your earring behind," I said.

"Yeah, it would have given the nurses a laugh." He smiled.

Despite our banter, both of us kept turning our eyes to the window, hearing the high whine of the wind and the lashing rain. When would it end? What was going to happen to us?

Bob tried to reassure me. "Don't worry. We'll be safe." He squeezed my hand, and I could read his thoughts. We'd been through a lot together over thirty-six years, and we'd get through this.

Hurricane Agnes in 1972 had been only our first crisis. We endured the terrifying morning trapped as flood-waters rose up our staircase, the rescue by boat, and then the depressing aftermath when we piled half our possessions in a heap at the curb, hosed out the house—literally—and fought the mold that climbed up our walls until winter. But that fright paled four years later, when a mole on Bob's back turned out to be melanoma. Hearing the dreaded word *cancer* cast the dark cloud of mortality over our summertime life. We were ignorant and didn't realize how deadly that form usually was. Driving home from the dermatologist's office, Bob was irate.

"He was such an alarmist," said Bob. "Me-la-NO-ma." He imitated the doctor's dramatic pronouncement. "He sounded like the voice in one of those horror movies, the Voice of Doom, trying to scare me."

"Well, it scares me," I said. "What did he say to do?"

"Surgery. If they don't cut it out, it could spread." Bob was still imitating the doctor. "'To the GROIN.' That horror movie voice again. Then his two nurses piped up in the background, 'To the groin, to the groin!' They sounded like the three weird sisters. I'm calling my doctor in Texas."

Bob's internist in Dallas, a long-time friend, referred us to a surgeon there, who cut a huge hunk out of Bob's back, and with it all the cancer cells. He pronounced Bob totally cured and sent him back to Pennsylvania with a six-inch incision held together by thick wire stitches cushioned in red vinyl tubes. Bob went back to teaching his classes, telling his students they were looking at the "bionic man." Weeks later, the university's physician removed the stitches in the field house while student athletic trainers looked on, getting a real-life lesson. Then our life got back to normal.

All was well for fourteen years. In 1990, the winds of mortality chilled us again. A new cancer had appeared, this time in Bob's bladder. Doctors said the cause was probably smoking, although we'd both quit for good five years before. But we learned that the small town where we lived had experienced a cluster of bladder cancer cases thought to be caused by the benzene left behind at a defunct chemical factory. It seemed possible that may have contributed to Bob's disease too, though doctors insisted smoking was the primary culprit. Whatever the cause, there was no question: we would fight.

Once again, surgery was the answer. In June of 1990, we returned to Dallas, where Bob went under the knife. The surgeon found no spread to lymph nodes and told us all the cancer cells had been removed. The threat was over.

"Let's go to New Orleans," said Bob. "I can recuperate there."

We had visited often and grown to love the Crescent City. So we made arrangements for an extended post-surgery stay, a stay that deepened our love for the city and made us resolve to live there one day. During four weeks in the blazing heat of July in the French Quarter, we dealt with the aftermath of the surgery and Bob slowly reclaimed his life.

Barely mobile at first, Bob walked a little more each day. We had celebratory dinners at Galatoire's and discovered the Palm Court Jazz Café. We heard Pete Fountain play at his club on the river. We got caught in afternoon rainstorms *á la* Tennessee Williams. Bob even fell victim to the legendary "shoe scam," taking a five dollar bet from a smiling teenager who approached, pointed to Bob's feet, and said, "Betcha' five dollars I can tell you where you got them shoes."

I could see the wheels turning as Bob thought, There's no way he'll guess Lock Haven, Pennsylvania. He took the bet. The answer came with high drama and a lilting cadence: "You got them shoes on your feet on Bourbon Street." Bob paid up, smiling sheepishly.

Over the course of those weeks, against a soundtrack of New Orleans jazz, we talked and laughed our way back to normalcy.

Now our goal was to get as close as we could to normalcy again—as soon as Katrina blew herself out. Finally, blow herself out she did. Late Monday afternoon, the rain slackened and the winds calmed. Streets outside the hospital slowly drained of water and dried. The sky turned blue, peppered with scudding clouds. As dusk fell, people walked dogs along the Clara Street sidewalks, and a few cars drove away. The air conditioning had stopped working when the power went off, but the generators kept fans blowing and air moving into the room, so the temperature wasn't too unpleasant. Bob's IV, powered by the generator, kept pumping. The phone in our room still worked, so we called family to report that the storm had been nerve-wracking but Katrina was over, and we'd survived.

Bob's face showed weariness from the anxiety of the day. He fell asleep early. The staff had worked hard to keep patients comfortable all through that long Monday, against the background of raging winds, the cacophony of kids' alternating laughter, whining, crying, chattering—and, at our end of the hall, incessant choruses of *Beauty and the Beast*.

I lay in the dark on my creaky cot, ready for sleep and thinking that the hurricane was a bad one, but not too bad. At least it was over. The lyric still echoed in my head: *Just a little change, small to say the least....* Maybe tomorrow we could go home. We'd finish the next chemo and get back to our life. We'd sit in our courtyard again. Bob could grow the orchids and stag head ferns he'd planned, and I could plant the gardenia I'd always wanted.

Chapter Three

Pools That Stand in Drains

Tuesday, August 30

In our room above Clara Street, we woke early. The sky outside was blue again, and the light from the rising sun shone in the northeast corner of our window. But the furious winds that had battered the hospital yesterday were a vivid memory, and outside Katrina had left a mess in her wake as she passed. The houses in surrounding neighborhoods looked wind-whipped, with pieces of siding blown off, roofs in tatters, fences down. Leaves, branches, upended trees, and other detritus from the storm littered the landscape. The white convertible was catty-corner in the street below our window, blown out of the parking lot and down the slope by the storm. Light poles leaned and power lines drooped across the length of Clara Street. At the far edge of the parking lot across the street, a fence made of aluminum strips wound into chain link had been whipped by the wind and flattened in sections. Strips of metal were peeled out, bent and flapping. It looked as if the fence had been attacked by a giant can opener.

Voices in the hospital's hall were cheerful, without the tension of yesterday, and when nurses came in on morning rounds, things seemed almost normal again. First a tall young nurse named LaShandra came in bringing Bob's morning pills.

"So you made it through Katrina, Mr. Perry," she said, handing Bob a cup of water. She had a quiet voice and a calm manner.

"Pretty wild, wasn't it?" said Bob. He swallowed the pills.

"Wild is right," said LaShandra. "Never been through a hurricane like that. I hope it's my last."

"Did you work all weekend?" I asked her.

"Since Saturday. Part of Team A, the first responders. Team B will come in soon to relieve us. I was glad to get the overtime, but yesterday was hectic with all the extra people here."

"Do you have family with you here?" I asked.

"I live with my mom. She evacuated to Texas when she found out I was going to work for the storm. So I know she's safe. What about you all?" She checked Bob's IV tubes.

"Just us. We're hoping Bob can be discharged soon. Then we'll go check on our house."

"Your nurse'll be coming in soon," said LaShandra. "She can tell you about discharge. Let us know if you need anything, Mr. Perry." She smiled at Bob as she turned toward the door.

After awhile, when Nurse Carolyn appeared, I asked her whether she thought Bob could go home today.

"We couldn't contact Dr. Veith yesterday in the storm, but we'll try again today. If he says it's okay, we can discharge you."

When I had spoken to our oncologist, Dr. Robert Veith, on Saturday, I'd asked him whether he thought we should evacuate. "I can't make that decision for you," he'd said. "My family left, but I'm staying. I think maybe it won't be as bad as they're predicting. Go to Memorial and get fluids, and then you can decide."

Although Dr. Veith had not been at the hospital during the storm, I knew the ER doctor had contacted him, so he knew Bob had been admitted. It was comforting to know he was still in town. An easygoing, gentle man, he had guided us both through the physical and emotional stresses of chemotherapy with wisdom, compassion, and a ready wit. We trusted and relied on him. As soon as they reached him, he would probably agree we could go home. Bob was better, I could tell. He was still weak, but that was expected with chemo—I hoped he would steadily improve until it was time for another dose next week.

Bob was becoming weary of the brutal cycles of drugs and the toll they took on his body. The chemicals were so toxic they had to be followed immediately with several liters of saline to flush the harsh drugs out of his system. Each time he had an infusion, the slow intravenous drip immobilized him for at least ten hours. Treatments made him weak and listless—at times it was hard to remember the vibrant, energetic man he'd been before. Bob had been reluctant to start the most recent round of chemo, but when the time came, he did. He was still determined to hit this cancer with every weapon possible.

Bob's breakfast tray came, scrambled eggs, a box of cereal with milk, coffee, and a bottle of Boost, a protein drink chemo patients often depend on. He ate a bit and drank the Boost, and again I ate some of the leftovers. Still hungry, I headed down to the cafeteria, hoping to find at least more coffee—I definitely needed a boost myself. The lobbies and waiting areas were still crowded and even more cluttered than yesterday. People's faces looked weary—they had spent an uncomfortable forty-eight hours and were ready to go home.

When I got to the basement, the floors were wet from yesterday's rainwater, but I made my way through the dark hallways. This part of the hospital showed its age: dull walls, exposed pipes, the clank and hum of machinery. Display cases plastered with artwork from the children's day care center—crayon drawings, blobby finger paintings in bright colors—attempted to enliven the entrance to the cafeteria, but today the place was dark and empty, except for a staff member (or perhaps he was a volunteer) working behind a counter lit by a lone bulb. He looked up and told me they were closed. "Food's been taken upstairs," he said.

I paused at a stand holding single-serving cereal boxes. "Could I just have one of these?"

He gave me a troubled, apologetic look. "No, we really have to save those for staff."

Right, typical, I thought. All the money we've poured into this hospital, and they can't let me buy a measly box of raisin bran? With the crowds of extra people in the hospital, I supposed they were trying to ration the food. Resigned and empty-handed, I returned to the third floor. We'd probably be getting discharged before long, and I could eat at home.

Back in our room, Bob and I wondered about the effect of yesterday's storm on the rest of the city. How long would it be before the streets were cleared of debris? Would we have trouble driving the few miles between the hospital and home? Going home still seemed the logical next step, and we speculated about how long the discharge process would take.

Bob had started chemotherapy in Houston, enrolled in a clinical trial at the M. D. Anderson Cancer Center. Later, his doctor there coordinated with Dr. Veith so that some chemo cycles could be done in New Orleans. We had soon discovered that *patient* was a good word for anyone undergoing cancer treatment. A huge part of our time was spent waiting: waiting for consultations, waiting for lab work, waiting for test results, waiting while cell-killing chemicals flowed into Bob's body. Lobbies and smaller waiting rooms throughout the M. D. Anderson clinic featured large aquarium tanks filled with bright angelfish, goldfish, clownfish and other fish swimming lazily through turquoise water. I'd catch Bob staring at them, a wistful look on his face.

In the past weeks and months of his chemo, when we had to spend a night at M. D. Anderson's hospital in Houston or here at Memorial each time the drugs were administered, Bob would chafe at the long waits for discharge, eager to get out. He'd grumbled that the paperwork and signatures required to get out of hospitals seemed double the number to get in. This time we weren't destined to get out of Memorial any time soon, but it wouldn't be the fault of paperwork.

Sometime mid-morning that Tuesday, I glanced out our window and saw a rivulet of water flowing down Clara Street, being pulled into the drains. This was odd. "There's water in the street," I said to Bob. "Wonder where it's coming from."

"That was a lot of rain," said Bob. "Maybe it's taking awhile to drain."

"But the streets were dry last night. It's strange," I said.

Nurse Carolyn walked into the room at that point, and I asked if she had any news about what was happening in the rest of the city. "You don't have a radio?" she said. "Just a minute—I'll get you mine." She left and returned with a small, battery-powered radio and said we could keep it for awhile. A radio was one thing I hadn't brought with us. Borrowing Carolyn's gave us what both of us were eager for: information. It was tuned to a local station that normally played jazz. Now it was all talk.

Over the next couple of hours, various nurses and a few strangers popped into our room to look out our windows, which must have had an especially good view— we could see almost the entire length of Clara Street below us, and in the distance the blocks of neighborhoods between the hospital and South Claiborne Avenue, looking in the direction of Lake Pontchartrain. There was very little movement on any of the streets, and the surrounding landscape looked battered from the winds. A wiry, intense-looking woman, who said she was the wife of a patient across the hall, was the first to pop her head in our door. "Somebody said there's water in the street—can I look out your window?" she asked, all in one breath. She was followed by a steady stream of others, some we recognized and most we didn't, all greeting us with a variation of those words.

Down on Clara Street, the volume of water had grown, and the drains were bubbling, a sign that they weren't able to handle the speed of the flow and were backing up. As we watched, the rivulet grew until it covered most of the street. From curb to curb, Clara Street became a rushing stream. Where was the water coming from?

No one knew, but it was getting deeper. The sun shone—a beautiful day had followed the storm. Probably the drains were full of debris from yesterday's winds, and that was the reason for the back-up. Still, the new water was puzzling.

On the radio, callers reported from other parts of the city. A woman called to say water was rising on Carrollton Avenue. "We didn't have this much water yesterday," she said. "What's going on?" No one knew. The announcers couldn't offer any answers. We didn't know it yet, but that lack of information would become one of the worst—and most dangerous—frustrations in the days to come.

The radio announcers told us that thousands of people had gathered in the Superdome for refuge. Early estimates varied wildly, from 9,000 to 20,000, and more people were arriving as they fled various parts of the city. The storm had peeled away a huge section of the structure's roof, the power was off, and there was little food or water, but people were not being allowed to leave because water was rising in the streets around the Dome. Even more alarming were the reports of looting downtown. One caller said the Winn Dixie supermarket near the edge of the French Quarter had been emptied. I'd passed it Sunday on my way back to the hospital, and it had been boarded up tight. Maybe people had broken in to get food and water. Another caller reported a rumor that some parts of the city were being deliberately flooded in order to "save the French Quarter." He said this rumor had caused anger and fueled the looting. The radio announcers tried gently to discount even the possibility that this could be true, but no one could offer a factual denial.

"Surely people can't really believe that," I said to Bob.

"Well, there's a certain history," he said. "It happened in the 1927 Mississippi flood, didn't it?"

That spring, weeks of unusual rains had swollen the Mississippi River, causing severe floods all along its path through the states of Louisiana, Mississippi, Arkansas, Kentucky, Tennessee, and as far north as Cairo, Illinois. As John M. Barry explains in *Rising Tide: The Great Mississippi Flood of 1927 and How It Changed America*, investors out of state were worried that New Orleans would be inundated as well. To reassure them, a local committee of wealthy business and political leaders called Citizens Committee for Flood Relief deliberately dynamited the levee, blasting downriver from New Orleans at Caernarvon, thirteen miles below Canal Street near the community of Poydras, and causing breaches that flooded St. Bernard and Plaquemines parishes. Randy Newman's song

"Louisiana 1927" memorializes that event: *Louisiana/ They're tryin' to wash us away, they're tryin' to wash us away*.... In the coming weeks and months, that song would be revived and become a kind of anthem in post-Katrina New Orleans.

Outside the hospital, a few people passed in the street, wading through water that was now knee-deep. A middle-aged black man came by pushing a metal shopping cart. In the cart, a little mouse-colored Chihuahua sat on top of a huge heap of soda and beer cans. The dog gazed around, looking fearful, as the man slowly plodded west, through the water.

By early afternoon, water was thigh-high for the occasional passer-by, and halfway up the doors of the white convertible, still sitting catty-corner in Clara Street. In the surrounding neighborhoods, as far as I could see, streets and yards were covered with water. Water crawled up steps and sloshed over porches of the one-story shotgun houses. Where was it all coming from? Now the radio began to mention vague reports that the levees had broken, that the giant pumps that drained New Orleans of rainwater weren't working, but those sounded like more rumors, spread by alarmists. Why would the levees break now, when the hurricane was over? The rain had stopped more than twelve hours ago, so how could the pumps be a problem?

Reports came in of more looting—people had broken into the shops on Canal Street, the wide avenue that divided the French Quarter and the Central Business District. A Walmart near the Lower Garden District was being ransacked. Fires had started at various places in the city. Smoke was reportedly billowing from a warehouse by the river. The radio hosts were having trouble getting confirmation, or any information, from authorities.

We were startled when the intercom in our room cackled with a sudden announcement: people on upper floors should now use toilets on the lower floors. Alarmed, I asked Bob, "What does that mean? Why would the toilets not work?"

"Maybe the upper floors aren't getting water pressure."

I checked at once. Thank heaven, our toilet worked.

Tension in the hospital, and especially in Room 3158, was rising.

At about 3:00 p.m., the intercom sputtered and another announcement boomed through the halls and into the room. "Attention, patients. Triage doctors will be visiting all patients shortly. All patients, please wait in your rooms. Triage doctors will be visiting you shortly."

Bob and I looked at each other. The word *triage* suggested war, or disaster, or at least an emergency. What could this announcement mean? I sat by his bed, both of us wondering and expectant.

Before long, a man wearing a doctor's white coat appeared at our door. He was young, dark-haired, and intense, with the tall, lanky build of an athlete. He greeted Bob by name and looked inquiringly at me. When I introduced myself as Bob's wife, he addressed us both and explained that since they couldn't contact Dr. Veith, he had been put in charge of Bob's care. "How are you feeling, Mr. Perry?"

"Better than I did three days ago," Bob answered.

"Good." He did a quick examination, and then said, "Well, I'm afraid I have some disturbing news. The water outside has been rising all day, as you know, and the hospital is flooding. The people in charge have decided we have to evacuate, so everyone will be leaving."

I had watched the water inching up all day, but the idea of evacuating the hospital had never entered my mind.

"When?" Bob asked.

"We're not sure. It might start tonight, but you'll probably go tomorrow. Patients will be taken out first, then family members, and the staff last."

"What do you mean?" I said. "Bob and I can go together, can't we?"

"No," he said, "we have to take patients out first, separately. You won't be able to go together."

It took several seconds for the enormity of what he was saying to sink in. When it did, my eyes filled with tears. My chest tightened. "But where will you take us?" I said. "Bob needs me with him. We have to stay together."

The doctor looked at me with genuine sympathy in his eyes. "I'm sorry. At this point we don't know where patients will be taken, probably to other hospitals. But it's not likely that you'll be able to go together."

I wasn't ready to accept this. How could they separate us, when Bob was so sick? For more than a year, I'd been going through every step of his illness and treatment with him, a partner through every test, every setback, every decision. I'd even had to learn to give him the blood-thinning injections he had to have daily, shots to his stomach muscle that had seemed impossible to me at first but now were routine—yet I knew he couldn't do those injections himself. Bob needed me. I had to stay with him.

"But Bob's in the middle of chemotherapy," I said. "Isn't there some way I can go with him?"

He shook his head sadly. "I'm sorry, no. The only alternative is to discharge him. If we discharged Mr. Perry, you could evacuate together, but it's not clear where you'd go. Perhaps to the Superdome. I don't really advise that. I don't think we should discharge your husband, he's still too ill."

I was silent, stunned. From what I had heard on the radio about conditions in the Superdome, I certainly didn't want either of us to go there. And how would we get anywhere, with water all around us? I knew the doctor's advice was right—Bob was still weak, and we surely couldn't face this flood on our own. We'd have to do what they told us to do. We really had no choice.

"Okay," I said. "I don't want you to discharge him. We'll stay. How will they take us out?"

"We're not sure. Some patients may go by boat. They'll probably take Mr. Perry by helicopter. We'll try to give you as much notice as we can before it's time for you to leave," said the doctor. "In the meantime, try to get some rest. As I said, it'll probably be tomorrow." He gave us a regretful smile and left.

I looked at Bob. His brow was furrowed, his eyes troubled. I was still standing by the door when a man in a Roman collar appeared. "I'm Father Marse," he said, "I'm a Catholic priest and hospital chaplain. Are you all right?" I guessed he had been following the doctor, a back-up in case people went to pieces at the news of the impending evacuation.

I was sure my face looked stricken, but I tried to sound calm. "Yes," I said. "I can't believe we won't be able to stay together, but we're okay."

"It's a bad situation," he said, "but I know they'll do everything they can to evacuate you safely. Let me know if you need anything. God bless you."

I thanked him, and he moved on down the hall. What we needed was to get out of here, I thought. Together.

I took a deep breath and turned to Bob. "I can't believe this is happening," I said. We'd feared the hurricane, but this was far worse. Memorial was no longer a shelter. Now the hospital was going to force us to leave, and to leave each other. We'd thought the danger had passed, but a new, far more frightening danger lay ahead. If I let myself, I knew I could fall apart, but I could not let myself. I couldn't risk making Bob too fearful or too upset. I had to stay calm and rational.

"Okay," I said, "If we're going to be separated, we've got to figure out a way to find each other."

"Call the family," Bob said. "Maybe they can help."

Our cell phone didn't work but the room phone did, so I placed a call first to Dallas, to our sister-in-law Nell, the widow of Bob's older brother Bill. A small blonde dynamo and the quintessential Texas matriarch, Nell was the center of the Perry network and had been in close touch all through Bob's treatment. I started describing the situation in a matter-of-fact voice, but when I got to the part about being separated, my voice broke and I ended up wailing. "They're making us leave and Bob and I can't go together, they're going to separate us. They can't tell us where they'll take him. I'm afraid I won't be able to find him." Nell was as stunned as I was and could do little more than commiserate and tell me she was sure we'd be okay. She promised to let Bob's brother George and her sons Billy and Randy know, and they would all help however they could. Next, I called my brother Bill in Raleigh. Six years younger than I and my only brother, Bill was always calm, wise, and able to deflect a crisis, usually with humor. He picked up on my panic at once.

"Carolyn, I'd drive there in a minute and come to get you both, but the roads into the city are closed—they're not letting any cars into New Orleans. Looks like we're going to have to wait 'til you're out."

"Well, I guess even if you could drive in you couldn't get here to the hospital—we're surrounded by water. It's like we're in the middle of a lake. I just wish we could go wherever they take us together."

Bill echoed Nell and said the family would all keep in touch with each other by phone and email and do everything they could to find out where we ended up. He made the practical suggestion that I charge our cell phone's battery and conserve it, since I might need it to make contact once we were out. After I said goodbye, I took his advice and attached our charger and cell phone to one of the red emergency plugs in the hall. The room phone was still working, so I called my sisters, Lorraine and Liz, who also tried to reassure me. But no matter how positive the family tried to be, those words *you can't go together* kept swirling in my head.

My adrenaline was pumping. Now I searched for action I could take, things I could do to help us. I didn't want to sit and simply wait, and I didn't want to cause Bob to get overly upset, which couldn't be good for him. Rather than focus on the evacuation, I looked around the room. "What's going to happen to all this stuff I brought to the hospital?" I asked him. "I'm sure I can't take all of it with us. What should I do with it?"

"I wondered why you lugged all that stuff up here," he said, a bit testily.

"Well, I didn't know whether the house might flood —I thought it'd be safer here. I should've left it, but bringing it here seemed smart at the time."

"Why don't you put it in the car?" Bob suggested.

"I wonder if I can still get to the car," I said. "I think I'll go and see."

Bob said he'd be all right for awhile if I left, so I made my way downstairs. The garage elevator had stopped working, so it was no longer possible to get directly from the hospital into the garage. Instead, from the second-floor lobby, I had to walk down one staircase and up another that allowed access into the garage, and from there I walked up the circular ramps to the seventh floor. The car was just as I'd left it, so I re-traced my steps. The stairwell was dark and musty. Only the open doors on the landings let some light penetrate the hot, murky air. My feet clanked on the metal stairs, and someone on an upper landing was talking to a barking dog. All of a sudden there was a yap and a loud clamor, and a large collie came crashing down a flight of stairs, caught herself on the landing, and stopped, panting. Thank goodness, the dog seemed to be okay, and the owner comforted her and led her the rest of the way down. The animals had been cooped up for days, just like the human captives stuck in Memorial. All of us were stressed.

I returned to the room and told Bob I thought it was a good idea to take a lot of our stuff to the car. "I wonder how much I'll be able to take with me."

"Nurse Carolyn came in while you were gone. She said you could take one bag."

"Some of the financial stuff I hate to leave. Should I try to take the computer?"

"For God's sake, just put it all in the car. Don't burden yourself trying to carry things," Bob said. He lay propped up in the bed, feet sticking out of the rumpled sheet, his arm still attached to the tube dangling from the bag of IV fluids. His voice had that slight edge it could get, like a sergeant issuing orders to the troops. It usually meant he was worried.

I searched the hallways and found a rolling cart that wasn't being used. I loaded it up with the laptop, camera, one of the file boxes, most of the clothes we'd brought, and a bag containing all of Bob's medical records that I'd been accumulating for more than a year. I held back the file box with financial papers, a few recent medical records, our prescription medicines, and my purse holding wallets, credit cards, and the bank envelope—I'd find a way to take those with me.

As I was rolling the cart toward the elevators, a man walked along and offered to help. He had a cheerful smile, a bald pate with a surrounding blonde tonsure, like the hair of a monk, and his eyes behind large glasses were bright with intelligence and compassion.

"You look like you could use some help," he said.

"I'm taking this stuff to the garage," I said. "I need to leave it in our car."

"You'll need help carrying all that. I'll come with you, be glad to." He smiled.

"Well, if you're sure you don't mind," I said. "Thanks."

I had no idea who he was, but the help was welcome. Together we rolled the cart onto one of the two hospital elevators that were still working and rode to the second floor. We had to leave the cart there, get to the garage through the stairwell, and carry our load, in the sweltering August heat, up the circular ramps to the car. On the way, I learned the man's name was Bill Quigley and he was the husband of one of the oncology nurses in the bone marrow unit. He was sheltering at the hospital and helping out however he could. He was also an attorney. He asked about us, and his interest gave me a chance to vent my anxiety.

"My husband needs to continue his chemo. I'm hoping he can get back to M. D. Anderson in Houston, where he started treatment and doctors know him. But nobody here can tell us where they'll take him, and they won't let me go with him. Do you know what the plans are for the evacuation?"

"Nobody knows anything," said Bill. "I think they're in touch with Tenet and they're trying to organize something. But I haven't heard any plan, just that everyone's got to leave." He helped me stow all the stuff in the trunk of our silver Honda in its spot near the top of the garage.

"I don't know what will happen to the laptop in this heat," I said, "but I guess I have to leave it. It's all just stuff." I slammed the trunk closed. "I'm really grateful for your help." My tee shirt stuck to my back, wet with perspiration. Lugging all that stuff up seven flights had been exhausting. Yesterday's winds were gone, and the deadening heat and humid August air made the garage swelter. This trip would have been quite a struggle without Bill's help.

On the way back down, we talked about the many family members who were volunteering to help the staff cope. Bill told me the basement was now flooded and all the food had been carried to an upper floor, where they'd set up a makeshift kitchen.

We walked together to the garage stairwell, which was dark and dusty in the late afternoon. A volunteer held a flashlight at the doorway, and Bill followed me down the stairs. As we walked, I turned back to tell him about the dog I'd seen fall down the stairs earlier. I was wearing rubber flip-flops, and as I talked, my foot caught on the next-to-last stair tread. I reached out to find balance but grasped only air—in an instant I felt myself falling, just like the dog. My forehead hit the concrete floor, my glasses cut into my eyebrow, my nose and lip scraped the rough concrete. I lay in the dark, hearing shouts of alarm from every direction.

Bill stood over me, telling me not to move. Almost immediately, I was surrounded by EMT types, warning me to be still, holding my head, flashing lights in my eyes. One wanted to put me on a backboard, but someone in scrubs said, "No, put her in this wheelchair."

Still stunned, I was helped to my feet, into a wheelchair, and rolled into the hospital. I took stock, and nothing seemed to be broken. We moved through hot hallways full of milling people, sprawled on floors and leaning against walls, all watching our progress curiously. "I'm okay, really," I protested. "Just let me get back upstairs to my husband."

The volunteer pushing the wheelchair had asked me my name. "You'll be okay, Miss Carolyn. We'll get you checked right away." He wheeled me into the ER, where I was greeted by the same dark-haired nurse named Erin who had been on duty when Bob and I arrived on Saturday. She helped me onto a bed, took my blood pressure, cleaned the cut over my eye, and told me the doctor would be right in.

"But my husband's a patient upstairs," I said. "They told me they don't know when the evacuation will start, and I don't want them to take him without me there. Please, I've got to go back."

"That eye needs some stitches," Erin said. "I remember you from before the storm. How's your husband doing?" She had a soothing bedside manner. She reminded me of the nurse who seemed to feature in every TV hospital drama, the nurse everyone relies on, who holds the ER together. Her eyes and smile were kind.

"He's better, but I know he's worried about being evacuated, and he'll be wondering where I am. I really need to get back."

Bill had followed me to the ER, and now he came into the room as the nurse left. "Don't worry," he said. "I'll go up and tell your husband where you are. You stay here and let them fix you up."

The cut was beginning to throb. I gingerly put my fingers over my eye and could feel the wet stickiness of blood in my eyebrow. "Okay. Bob's in room 3158. Please tell him I'm okay and I'll be there as soon as I can. Tell him not to worry. And thank you, Bill." I later learned that Bill Quigley's role as messenger extended beyond helping me and Bob. In the ensuing days, he was one of the few people who were able to use email and a still-working cell phone to contact the outside world and tell them of Memorial's plight.

The nurse came back and attached a vinyl ID bracelet around my left wrist. She was followed by the same dark-haired young doctor who had visited our room earlier and told us the news of the evacuation. Now he was wearing green scrubs and a sweatband. The staff was apparently taking on multiple roles—most had been working continuously for three days. As he stitched up the cut over my eye, I gathered they were a couple because they talked about their dog, an Irish setter ensconced on the fifth level of the garage.

"What's going to happen to the animals?" I asked.

"They're not going to let people take pets when they evacuate," he said, "so I don't know. One of us will have to stay behind. We can't leave without the dog." He gave me a

51

prescription for antibiotics, told me to fill it once I got out of the hospital, and asked me to wait—someone would be back to give me a tetanus shot. They left, discussing the feeding schedule for their dog.

I waited, sitting on the ER gurney. After spending weeks in and out of hospitals with Bob over the past sixteen months of his cancer treatments, both here and in Houston, suddenly now I was a patient, being tended to by stalwart caregivers who were trying not to be distracted by the rising water, the impending evacuation, family members possibly stranded in the wings of the hospital or somewhere else in the flood, and the prospect of leaving caged pets behind—all while trying to focus on the patients in their care. Who of us could have imagined when we came to this place three days ago that now we would all be marooned, trapped by rising waters, and facing who knew what?

As I left the ER Tuesday afternoon, I saw a crowd of people congregated on the raised outside ramp, where ambulances normally delivered patients. Now it had become a loading ramp. The water had risen too high for trucks, so boats would have to pull up to the ramp, but I didn't see any sign of a boat. People stood on the ledge waiting, staring out, the water lapping just inches below their feet.

Later, when a nurse said to me as I was waiting for evacuation, "Oh, you're the Code Sprint," I learned that was the code used when someone fell on hospital property. Somehow, the word *sprint* didn't seem the best way to describe my moves on that staircase.

"Code Klutz is more like it," I said.

When I got back to our room, Bob was relieved to see me. Bill Quigley had visited him and explained where I was, and when Bob's nephew Randy, Nell's son, called soon after from Dallas, Bob told him I'd fallen but he didn't know how badly I was hurt. Now, seeing the bandage above my eye, he clasped my hand and pulled me closer, brushing my hair back gently so he could inspect the eye. "Uh, oh," he said. "You're going to have a shiner for sure."

"I know," I said. "I scraped my glasses on the concrete, but at least they didn't break. There's a big scratch on one lens, but I'll still be able to see. I guess I'm lucky I didn't injure my eye or break a leg."

Randy had said most of the family's calls into the hospital were not getting through—he'd been surprised when Bob answered. "Maybe we can still call out." I picked up the phone by Bob's bed, and it still had a dial tone. I punched in my brother's number and was relieved to hear him answer.

My sister Liz had contacted a friend working with Emergency Services in California, and now my brother relayed her message: "Liz's friend Eileen says find out the name of the person in the hospital in charge of disaster response. Having a name can help you to know who to talk to and help us to find you, too. She said to record all the numbers on Bob's ID bracelet and let us know them. Those numbers can help us to track him down. Also, be sure to list all the family's names and phone numbers in Bob's medical chart. That chart will stay with him when they take him out."

"That all makes sense," I said. "I'll do it right away."

"Eileen also said if worse comes to worst and the plumbing fails, try to get some plastic bags—you can line your toilet and periodically throw away the bags."

"Oh, God," I said to my brother, "I hope it doesn't come to that."

"We're all in touch by email," Bill went on. "We'll try to find out where they take Bob. I'm glad you're not hurt badly." I could hear the worry in his voice. "Maybe now they'll consider you officially a patient, and you'll be able to go with him. Call us when you can."

I gave him the numbers from both our ID bracelets and told him I would try to call again with the name of Memorial's disaster planner. I hung up and walked to the nurses' desk. They all immediately asked about the stitches above my eye, and Carolyn jokingly asked who had socked me. She let me record the family's phone numbers in Bob's medical chart, and another nurse told me Susan Mulderick was the designated disaster coordinator. Returning to the room, I made one more call to give this information to my brother. Bill told me the TV reports now confirmed that levees and flood walls had collapsed and water was pouring into the city. Plans to plug the breaches with sandbags dropped by helicopter were underway. No one knew how long repairs would take.

At approximately 5:30 p.m., the phone in our room went dead. With no cell phone and now no land line, we were cut off.

Darkness gathered. The water was still rising. By Tuesday evening, the hospital's phones were all down. The radio had become a lifeline, our only source of news from outside. The station was headquartered in downtown New Orleans, and the announcers talked about how dark it was with power out all over the city, and how bright the stars seemed overhead. There were sporadic reports of violence and more looting, but no one could offer definitive details.

I stared out our large window at the blackness stretching as far as I could see. The white convertible seemed to float in the dark water. The small shotgun houses, built close together, formed dark silhouettes in the distance, with no lights in windows. In the part of the sky I could see, stars glimmered. Nothing moved except the water, heaving slightly with the currents, and all outside was silent.

In the hospital, the children in the halls were restless, into their third day of being cooped up. But friendships were forming, and some of the older children were trying to entertain the younger ones. Outside our room, a boy about ten huddled with two smaller boys, telling them a string of what he called "stupid jokes" and causing high-pitched giggles at the answers to the "Knock Knocks." The same little girl, a blond with purple bows tied to pony tails above each ear, was playing *Beauty and the Beast*—still:

> *Ever just the same, ever a surprise,*
> *Ever as before, ever just as sure as the sun*
> *   will rise.*
> *Just a little change....*

"I wonder how long that battery will last," I said to Bob.

"May the end come soon," he replied.

The staff seemed jittery and increasingly frazzled, but they went about their duties calmly. They too had been captive, sleeping in shifts on cots in communal rooms during their "off" times, no doubt worrying about how their loved ones or homes were faring. Yet they worked hard, tending to patients and trying to keep everyone's spirits up. We finally fell asleep with no more information about the evacuation, only that it would start tomorrow.

I was used to being awakened in the middle of the night, routine procedure in most hospitals. But this time, when nurses came in the early morning hours to check on Bob, they came in a group, and the only light came from flashlights they carried. Two nurses held big flashlights in upraised arms, shining light over Bob while a third checked his vital signs. The generators had shut down, electricity was off, and the hum of the fan blowing air into the room had stopped. The temperature was rising, and it wasn't possible to open the windows. For now, Bob's IV continued to run on emergency battery power, but I wasn't sure for how long. I didn't try to flush our toilet for fear that it wouldn't fill again—I would save that last flush for morning.

Chapter Four

Cone of Uncertainty

Wednesday, August 31

I slept fitfully and woke early. Sunlight tinged the eastern sky with pink—it was going to be another bright summer day, the second since the grey fury of Katrina passed over us. Outside our window, water still surrounded the hospital, glinting in the sunlight and deeper than yesterday. In the distance, houses were half-submerged, with water lapping across first-floor windows and doors. Only the top parts of the equipment in the playground across the street were visible: the swings were underwater. Cars parked in the street, including the white convertible, seemed to float, with water covering their hoods and inching toward their roofs. The owner of the white convertible had parked it with its top down. The red interior had been soaked by Katrina's rain, and now the rising flood would soon pour in. The water swirling in the street was blacker and dirtier than yesterday, with oil slicks on the surface and currents visible.

Bob woke when a young woman in shorts and rumpled tee-shirt carried in his breakfast tray and wished us a cheery "Good morning." With the generators down, all elevators had stopped, so getting food to patients on upper floors was a challenge. Volunteers were carrying trays up and down staircases, looking weary and hot.

"Try to eat some breakfast, hon," I told him. "You're going to need your strength today."

"Wow, your eye is about four colors," Bob said. "Does it hurt?"

"Not much." I looked in the mirror above our sink and sure enough, there were purple streaks below my left eye and bluish-red blotches under the stitches and above the eyelid, with a tinge of yellow at the edges. Definitely a shiner.

Bob picked at his food but didn't eat much of it, and I couldn't either. No fan moved the air, and the room was stifling and hot. My stomach was in knots. What would the day bring?

Not long after breakfast, we heard the first loud *thwack, thwacks* of a helicopter outside our window, banking toward the roof. Soon Nurse Carolyn came in and told us to relax, we had a wait. The critical babies on the sixth floor were going to be flown out first, then they would work their way down the floors. Since we were on three, it would be awhile before they'd get to Bob.

"Are the mothers going with the babies?" I asked.

"I don't think so," said Carolyn. "They'll have nurses with them in the 'copters because they need constant care." Those poor mothers—I could imagine how frightening it would be to watch their new infants fly away and not know where they'd be taken.

I'd piled our remaining belongings at the foot of my cot: one file box full of important papers, my shoulder bag containing wallets and bank pouch with cash, and a canvas tote full of notebooks, medical records, and our medications, including a plastic bag holding a fifteen-day supply of pre-filled syringes, the blood-thinning injections Bob needed daily. Each syringe full of medicine had cost roughly $90. And I certainly didn't want to leave them behind.

When a doctor at M. D. Anderson had told me Bob needed daily injections and I'd have to learn to give them, my reaction was cold fear. I fled the room, walking the halls for long minutes, wondering how I could possibly stick three-inch needles into my husband's stomach.

A nurse met me when I returned to the room, calmly assuring me that of course I could do it. She opened a practice kit, showed me the technique, and watched while I practiced injecting a syringe into a foam cushion. Bob looked on warily.

"Okay, you've got it," said the nurse. "Now let's see you do it."

My hand shook as I pulled the plunger to fill the syringe then held it in one hand, compressing a section of Bob's stomach muscle with the other. My own stomach clenched.

"Good," said Bob. "Go ahead." Taking a deep breath, I pushed the needle into his flesh and depressed the plunger, watching the liquid slowly drain from the syringe. I looked at him fearfully.

Bob put his hand on my arm and smiled. "You're good," he said. "Didn't hurt at all." I didn't believe him, but I breathed.

Those daily shots became a ritual. Mottled bruises appeared on his stomach, and he sometimes winced with pain or complained: "Not there! That's sore."

More often he teased me. "Here comes my needle-wielding wife," he'd say, "always trying to drug me." I couldn't wait for the day when we could stop the injections, but until then I made sure we kept a supply of syringes ready, and I'd brought some to the hospital.

Now, eying the pile of belongings at the foot of my cot, Nurse Carolyn asked, "What's all that?"

"That's what I'm going to take. I can strap my purse around me and carry the file box and tote bag in each hand."

"No way," she said. "They're not going to let you on a helicopter or boat with all that. There won't be space. It's too much to carry."

"But what'll I do with it? It's all stuff we need."

"Give me the file box, the tote, and the bag of syringes," said Carolyn, sounding like a drill sergeant. "I'll put them in the staff room for now, then I'll take them home with me. I'll keep them safe, and when you get back to town, you can call me and get them. Here's my phone number. My house is not far from the hospital." She wrote her name, number and address on a notepad by Bob's bed.

The file box contained a wealth of personal information, including financial. I thought about the field day some identity thief could have with that box. But what choice did I have? I put as many of the prescription bottles as would fit into my purse, and I pulled out a few of Bob's medical records and some recent tax and other papers.

Those I would carry and the rest I'd entrust to Carolyn. I hated to leave the pre-filled syringes, but I supposed Bob could get that medicine wherever they took him, and we could use these syringes eventually. "Okay, if you're sure you don't mind," I said. "Thanks for offering."

Much later, I realized how illogical this whole plan was. What made us think Carolyn would be able to carry my things out when I couldn't? What made us assume either of us would be coming home anytime soon? Still, her offer was emblematic of the way all the hospital staff were trying to help the people in their care.

While we waited, the radio carried desperate voices of callers begging for help. The announcers tried to reassure and calm them but couldn't say when help would arrive. A woman wailed that she and her two children were stuck with an elderly neighbor on their rooftop and had been there since yesterday—what should they do? Stay there, the announcer told her, boats would be coming by. The water had crept slowly up our staircase when Agnes hit us back in June of '72. When it inched toward the sixth step, we decided we had to leave our townhouse and began to wave out our second-floor window, trying to signal a rescue boat. We'd had a roof over our heads and time to form a plan. Apparently the water from the several New Orleans levee breaches and floodwall failures had poured over the banks of the lake and canals, surging into houses and filling them in minutes, forcing people to scramble to their roofs in panic. Now they were stranded on the hot shingles, surrounded by floodwaters as the glaring August sun beat down.

The voices on the radio announced places where people still in the city should go and wait, if they could get there: the Superdome (although water still surrounded it), various overpasses on Interstate 10. Supposedly from these gathering spots, people would somehow get a way out of town. Would Bob or I end up in one of those waiting crowds? The announcers said the Causeway across Lake Pontchartrain was closed, the twin spans across the lake on I-10 going east were closed, I-10 itself was flooded in places. The only way out of the city seemed to be the

Crescent City Connection, the bridge over the Mississippi River to the West Bank. Yet there were reports by callers that people were being stopped on the bridge by armed guards, who forced them to turn back. Radio announcers tried to confirm these reports but could get no official information. Later, we learned that tourists stuck in the city and groups of residents—many of them black—had walked over the bridge, trying to escape the flooded city. They were turned back at gunpoint by Jefferson Parish police, who told them the West Bank had no facilities to help them.

At Memorial, the water continued to rise, reaching to the bottom edge of an octagonal stop sign at the end of Clara Street, beneath our window. That meant the flood was nine feet deep outside the hospital. Cars were submerged in swirling, inky water. The faintly glowing outline of the white convertible looked eerie under the dark currents. Every once in awhile, a boat passed through what had been the street, mainly small motorboats or rowboats holding one or two people. At one point, a large airboat with what looked like a giant electric fan at its stern, the kind of boat pictured in brochures for swamp tours or scenes from movies set in marshlands, rounded the corner and roared down Clara toward Napoleon, dodging cars in its path and kicking up a huge wake. The boat was big enough to hold a lot of passengers, but only two people rode in it: the driver, and a guy standing in the bow with a large video camera on his shoulder, filming as they floated.

"That boat needs to be commandeered," I said to Bob. "It could hold a lot of patients."

The camera had the NBC logo on its side. Why didn't they stop at the hospital and load the boat with people? I wondered. Why are they letting empty boats with only photographers pass this hospital by? Don't those men realize this hospital is full of patients who need to get out? Why don't they bring us help instead of taking pictures? But the boat roared by.

Finally, about 11:00 a.m. Carolyn and a tall nurse named Andrea came in. Andrea was sunny and energetic, with wavy auburn hair cut short. She had tended to Bob a few times while we waited and told us about her golden retriever, who was not happy cooped up in the garage. They were rolling a wheelchair and Andrea chirped cheerily, "Okay, Mr. Perry, let's get you out of here."

Bob answered, mustering equal cheer: "I agree, let's do. Out of here sounds good to me."

They disconnected his IV. The bags of fluid were nearly empty, and the IV battery wouldn't last much longer anyway. They helped Bob into the wheelchair. I'd put our papers in a plastic bag that I folded into a packet and stuffed into the waistband of my slacks. The nurses rolled Bob's wheelchair out the door of 3158 and down the hall, with me trailing behind, carrying my purse and trying to keep the bulky envelope of papers secure at my waist as I walked. When we got to the end of the third-floor hall, Carolyn and Andrea said goodbye and wished us luck. I thanked them and wished them well, too, not expecting to see either of them again. None of us realized how much more time we'd be spending together.

The stairwell was full of both staff and volunteers, some in scrubs and some in shorts and tee-shirts, most looking tired and sweaty. They had an assembly line going. Patients in wheelchairs were lifted down, chairs and all, or transferred to sheet slings and lifted carefully down the flights of stairs. Though Bob had lost weight with chemo, his 6' 2" frame still carried about 175 pounds, so it took several people to maneuver him down the stairs in the chair. I held my breath as I walked behind, praying they wouldn't drop him.

We emerged into a large crowd of people in the second floor lobby, patients in wheelchairs accompanied by caregivers, all massed in one area near what had been the elevator to the Magnolia garage. With the elevator not working and the ground level of the hospital under nine feet of water, the normal entries to the garage were blocked. A hole about four feet in diameter had been knocked open in a brick wall between the hospital and the garage. The floor was littered with dirt and chips of mortar, and a couple of jagged bricks stuck out at the corners of the opening. Patients were being lifted one by one through the hole, and the family members accompanying them were climbing behind them into the darkness beyond the wall.

When it was our turn, several young men lifted Bob gently out of the wheelchair onto a backboard then moved him through the hole. I stooped over and followed, and a few feet into the garage a pickup truck waited. The men put Bob into the bed of the truck, stretched out next to another patient, and I was directed to squeeze into the back seat with several other people. The driver turned and addressed us all cheerily, "Everybody on board?" A brawny volunteer in shorts knelt with the patients in the back and knocked a signal on the window. "All set?" said the driver. "Magnolia Express. Here we go." The truck began to move slowly up the circular ramps.

"Do you know where we're going?" I asked a man riding shotgun.

"We're taking you to the eighth level. You'll go further up to the roof when helicopters come." The people in the truck were determinedly upbeat. I knew they must be tired, hot, and worried, but it didn't show. It felt good to be finally moving.

The truck stopped on level eight, almost the top of the Magnolia garage. Bob and the other man riding in the cab were helped into wheelchairs. Other patients were already there, some looking very ill; a few lay on pallets, some on gurneys with wheels, and others in wheelchairs. I wheeled Bob to the side of the garage with a half-wall, so we could look out and also catch any breeze that might stir the humid air. Even though the temperature was high and would get higher as the day wore on, it was a relief to be out of the stuffy, unventilated hospital room. At least we could breathe outside air, hot and sticky though it was.

A few armless hard-backed chairs had been scattered around the sides of the garage, and I moved one over so I could sit near Bob. The radio in our room had mentioned that supplies of drinking water were getting low in the city, so I was relieved when two young men carried several flats of plastic bottles and stacked them at the side of the ramp. Apparently Memorial had plenty of water. I was already parched in the sweltering heat, and though there was no way to chill the water, even tepid it was refreshing. From then on, I tried to make sure Bob and I both had a bottle handy.

Nurses and volunteers came and went, walking past us, up another level, and then up a metal staircase to the roof. When one of them passed by to check on the patients in our group, I tried again to find out what was going to happen.

"Are helicopters coming soon?" I asked.

"We think so," the nurse answered. "Some patients've already been taken up to the roof and they're waiting up there. Once they leave, we'll take another group up." Later, I learned that the old helipad at Memorial Hospital had not been used in more than ten years—at first, staff weren't even sure it could take the stress of a helicopter landing. But there was no other option.

"We heard the hospital's phones are all down," I said. "How are people communicating?"

"I think they're using satellite phones to the outside, and we have to use runners to relay messages here," she said. "It's a problem."

We all later realized what an understatement that was. Communication was a major problem city-wide, and contact among hospital staff, police, rescue groups, and everybody else had broken down almost totally. All day Tuesday, the radio announcers had lamented the lack of contact between officials, rescuers, and people who were trapped. In the days following, the communication problems got worse.

We hadn't been waiting long when we heard the loud *thwack, thwack* of a helicopter approaching. We couldn't see it, but the sounds thundered directly overhead as it landed on the roof. After awhile, the motor roared as the 'copter lifted off and banked to the side. Clouds of thick dust blew in, blowing my short hair straight out on end, showering all of us with grit and forcing us to close our eyes and turn away. As the roar diminished and the 'copter flew off into the distance, the dust settled and the garage got quiet again. The hot, muggy air was still. A smell of acrid dirt and oil and sweaty bodies began to permeate the garage.

I talked with a young man sitting on a chair nearby. His dark hair brushed his collar; he had a muscular build and a stoic expression. "Are you a patient?" I asked him.

"No, I was here with my uncle. They took him out last night, but I couldn't go with him."

"How did he leave?" I asked. "By helicopter?"

"No, some patients left last night in boats. They took one truck load, too, before the water got too high. My uncle was in pretty good shape, and the people who left with him in the boat were all able to walk. But they could only take patients—no family."

"Do you know where they took him?" I asked.

"No idea. I guess somewhere to high ground. And from there I hope to another hospital or shelter. I'll have to track him down as soon as I get out—whenever that'll be." He sighed.

Although Bob and I couldn't hear them, last night in addition to boats, some helicopters from a private ambulance service had landed and flown some critically ill patients out. Everyone expected they'd be back today to continue the evacuation.

We waited. As the morning lengthened, the temperature rose. At least we're high up and getting a little breeze, I thought. Still, the garage was beginning to bake. A sheen of perspiration covered my arms and mixed with the fine layer of grit from the helicopter. When another helicopter landed and soon took off, another cloud of dirt enveloped us.

Sometime mid-day, we heard a different sound, the far-off buzzing of a jet plane. Off in the distance, out the front of the garage looking towards the Mississippi, the silver glint got larger as the plane flew lower. When it swooped by Memorial, two nurses stood by the wall, pointing up and exclaiming, "Look, it's Air Force One!"

One of the radio voices had said President Bush had finally decided to cut short his vacation in Crawford, Texas, to fly over and get a look at the stricken Gulf coast. Apparently he was getting a fast glimpse of flooded New

Orleans, too. If I'd followed my instincts, I would have stood up, shaken my fist, and yelled at him: "Send us some help!" But I stayed quiet. I didn't want to alienate anyone around us who might help to get us out—besides, it was too hot for yelling. Instead, I sat and stewed, wondering why no rescuers were coming to help us. Later, much would be said and written about the President's flyover. Like the ship that passed by the drowning Icarus, Air Force One "had somewhere to get to and sailed calmly on." The photo of Mr. Bush gazing out the plane window from his cushy quarters 2500 feet above drowning New Orleans became an indelible image of his cluelessness and the botched federal response to the disaster, a flood that was the fault of flawed design, shoddy construction, and poor maintenance on federally-built levees.

I turned my attention back to Bob. He'd slumped further down in the wheelchair, and he'd gotten quiet. "How're you feeling? Are you okay, hon?"

Bob squirmed in the chair. He lifted one hip, grabbed the armrests, and tried to re-position himself. "This chair is the pits," he said. He'd been given a well-used wheelchair: the vinyl sling-seat was frayed, with no padding. One of the chair's footrests was missing, the other broken. "You'd think they could at least give me a chair with all its parts."

Something about the inflection he gave that word *parts* conjured up long-ago writing classes of Bob's I had observed over the years. Warning students against the common grammar error known as dangling participles, Bob always called them "dangling parts," uttering the phrase with high drama and exaggerated emphasis, never failing to elicit giggles and bawdy asides from the students. They usually remembered the lesson. This chair's footrest dangled on the ground and didn't support anything.

"I know," I said now. "Reminds me of dangling parts." That got a half-smile. "In a minute I'll see if I can get you another chair."

"I wish we could just get out of this place," he replied.

It was lunchtime. A nurse came walking around the corner of the ramp, carrying a tray of sandwiches. She stopped in front of Bob. "Want a sandwich, sir? I have ham or cheese."

"No, thanks" he said. "I'd take a Bloody Mary if you offered, though."

"Don't I wish!" She smiled. "Are you sure I can't sell you on a sandwich, or some crackers?"

He shook his head, and I declined too, although I did take a pack of cheese crackers. As the nurse walked on across the ramp toward another patient, Bob turned to me. "A ham sandwich would just about send me over the edge right now. All I want is to lie down. This chair's so damned uncomfortable. How much longer, I wonder?"

His gown, tied in back at the waist and snapped at the neck, had bunched up under one hip. I tried to loosen and smooth it. "I don't know," I said, "but I hope not long." One of Bob's literary specialties was revenge tragedy—I wondered what imaginary plots he might be concocting now. We were both sweating in the humid heat of the smelly garage. I handed him a bottle of water and urged him to drink. When were they going to get us out of here?

The interval since the last helicopter lengthened. We waited. The oppressive heat covered us like a blanket. I knew there were no working toilets anywhere. The staff who came by periodically warned us all to drink water so we wouldn't get dehydrated. Bob took a few sips now and then. After months of intense focus on Bob's physical state, I had become attuned to nuances and was often able to predict his reactions. I suspected he was afraid to drink too much for fear of triggering nausea.

I touched his arm and added my entreaties. "Please try to drink. You've just had three days of fluids, and you don't want to get dehydrated again."

"Madame Sosostris had a very bad cold..." was all he said.

I had to smile. "Yeah, and it turns out August is the cruelest month." No wonder T. S. Eliot came to mind. The sweltering Magnolia garage had become a scene in a new American *Waste Land*, and we were in it, dead center.

When I was in college reading *The Waste Land* for the first time, my friends and I used its opening line "April is the cruelest month..." to commiserate as we crammed for spring final exams in the heedless innocence of youth. The last time I'd thought of those words was April 30, 2004. That was the Friday morning the phone call from Bob's doctor had blindsided us: the results of a biopsy showed a tumor, a "bad one." In the time it took to utter that statement, our world turned upside down.

Earlier that April, what we had thought was flu turned out to be a urinary infection that landed Bob for the first time in Memorial Hospital. His internist, Dr. Brobson Lutz, stopped the infection but was puzzled by its cause, so he called in a specialist. After his melanoma in 1976 and his bladder surgery in 1990, Bob had been cancer-free for fourteen years, so the urologist suspected a kidney stone, but he scheduled a biopsy "just to rule out a tumor." Several days later, the phone call came. A new cancer, this one a rare form not often seen in New Orleans.

"Am I a goner?" asked Bob the next day, in the doctor's office.

Dr. Lutz answered, "I don't know" and urged us to head for M. D. Anderson Cancer Center in Houston, where specialists had experience with this uncommon type of what was called transitional cell carcinoma.

Bob called at once, and two weeks later we were on the road to Texas. Surgery wasn't an option this time, so Bob entered a clinical trial and began eighteen weeks of a "new and promising" chemotherapy. The powerful drugs sapped Bob's strength and energy, but he fought hard. We had some difficult times. He hated the thought of a blood transfusion and resisted fiercely. The night he had to give in and watch three bags of blood flow into his veins was a low point. Each scan or MRI meant hours or days of tension, wondering whether the verdict would be thumbs up or down. But we both stayed inherently hopeful. We wore our yellow LIVESTRONG bracelets. When doctors cited percentages, we stayed positive: Bob would be among the per cent who survived.

At the end of the first cycle, the M. D. Anderson doctor arranged to coordinate the next round of chemo with Dr. Veith in New Orleans. Every two weeks, Bob and I checked into Memorial Hospital for an overnight stay, during which three different drugs were pumped slowly into his veins, followed by several liters of saline to flush the chemicals immediately out of his system. In between treatments, he often had extra saline infusions in the doctor's office, to fight dehydration. Each session meant hours of immobility, tethered to IV tubes.

Finally, in October 2004, after another six-week cycle in Houston, tests showed the chemotherapy had worked—all signs of cancer were gone. Bob still suffered some lingering effects—he was weak, and one drug had damaged the nerves in his feet, making them numb—but we hoped those conditions were temporary. He was slowly feeling himself again. We took short walks around the French Quarter neighborhood and along the river. We flew to a family gathering at my sister Liz's home in Oakland. We laughed more. Life began to feel normal.

That holiday season we celebrated with special fervor. When snow fell on Christmas Day in New Orleans for the first time in fifty years, we watched the white flakes coat our ginger leaves and took it as an omen of hope. We looked forward to the coming springtime, with its festivals and rituals, and to a new April, "...breeding lilacs/ Out of the dead earth."

As we sat now in Magnolia, nurses I didn't recognize walked through the steamy garage frequently to check on patients, moving slowly from one to another. Some patients required attention, but others simply waited, or slept. No one around us seemed in acute distress. The level of the garage we were on was covered, but the afternoon sun beat in at the sides, and the August temperature and humidity made the garage swelter—I knew it was at least in the high 90s and it felt even hotter. I tore a piece of cardboard from one of the flats of water and used it as a fan, trying to stir up a dusty breeze on Bob and occasionally fanning myself. The helicopters had stopped coming. No one knew why. We waited.

Bob appeared more and more cramped and fatigued. His shoulders slumped and he shifted in the wheelchair, unable to get comfortable. I tried to distract him with conversation, speculating softly about some of the people in the group around us, wondering what their stories were. At least he's free of that IV tube, I thought.

He'd endured scores of IV needles over the past year, each puncturing various veins, which the nurses kept saying, accusingly, were "thin"—as if it were somehow his fault. They'd tried to install what was called a "central line," but Bob's body reacted—his upper arm swelled to twice its size—and the line had to be removed. Each time they drew blood or started an IV to administer chemo or fluids, finding a vein got more difficult, and finally Bob learned to preempt their fussing by announcing in his forceful voice, "I'm a difficult stick" and calling for the skilled IV Team, who always managed to find a vein. One day, he had to have another blood transfusion, something he always dreaded, but the IV Team nurse who appeared took his mind right off needles and blood.

She was a pillowy, middle-aged woman shaped like an apple and covered completely in cows. Printed on her scrub pants and smock, over a blue and pink background, were black and white and brown cows of varying sizes: big cows, small cows, smiling cows and sleeping cows. Two matching black and white heifer earrings dangled from her ears, and she wore a necklace and bracelet of linked plastic cows. Her dark hair was pulled into a pony tail, secured with two cow barrettes and tied with a very large bow, black and white in a pattern of cowhide. Bob took it all in, his eyes wide and a fascinated expression on his face. I caught his eye and bit my bottom lip to control my face.

"You must be fond of cows," said Bob.

"Oh, I am. Cows are cute, aren't they?" the cow-lady said cheerfully as she stuck the needle in his arm and attached the tube snaking up to the bag of dark red blood. After she left, we got a fit of the giggles and laughed off and on through the whole transfusion.

That was the exception, though. Usually the sight of another IV made both of us cringe.

I was about to try to lighten his mood by reminding him of the cow lady when suddenly a loud crash sounded outside the garage. Several of us moved over to the side to look. The legs of a chair had come crashing out one of the hospital windows on the third floor. The dark glass was shattered and the chair suspended, its legs sticking out. Then somebody pushed from inside and the chair fell into the murky water, now nearly ten feet deep. The muddy splash rose high against the building's brick façade. The hospital's windows were designed not to open, and with the air conditioning off for more than two days, the rooms must have been stifling. Someone desperate for air had used the chair to smash open the window, leaving jagged shards of smoky glass gaping.

Around 3:00 p.m., with no one moving from our group and no sign of any more helicopters, a woman rounded the corner, coming up the ramp from below. She walked over to a central position and looked around at all of us. Somewhat stocky, she was wearing the white coat of a doctor over her green scrubs, a white coat that had lost its starch and was wrinkled. Her dark hair was pulled behind her ears. Hands in pockets, she spoke to us all, saying she was a doctor but "not in charge." She wanted us to know that helicopters had stopped coming because they were being sent to other hospitals "where there are sicker patients." There may be more 'copters, she didn't know. They were trying to get us out, but we must be patient. Her tone seemed patronizing, and it irritated me. But I was glad at least to get some information, however meager—the first in about five hours. We waited some more.

Wednesday afternoon lengthened and Bob slumped further down in the wheelchair. He looked miserable. I started to fan him again, but in a few minutes, he looked up at me and in a quiet voice said, "I don't think I can do this anymore."

"Oh, Bob, please, you've got to hang on. We've got to get out of here. I'll see if I can find you a cot so you can lie flat." I walked over to two nurses across the ramp.

"Can I go downstairs and try to find a cot or gurney?" I asked. "My husband really can't sit in that wheelchair any longer—he needs to lie down."

One shook her head. "Sorry, no, there aren't any more gurneys. You stay here. I'll see what I can do, but we don't have many gurneys out here, and the few we have are being used." She was a nurse I didn't recognize, and her words were polite but curt, so I didn't have high hopes.

I walked back to the chair by Bob. "They say there aren't any gurneys, but they'll see what they can find. Hang in there, honey—surely this can't go on much longer." I stood behind the wheelchair and massaged his shoulders. He didn't react. Perspiration dotted his temples.

In a few minutes, the other nurse came over and asked Bob if he'd like to lie down. He nodded, and she helped to ease him out of the wheelchair and over to a mattress on the floor, at the front end of the garage. She'd covered it with a crisp sheet from a pile nearby. He sank onto it gratefully. I was relieved to see him more comfortable, but I was troubled. I had seen another patient lying on this mattress all day, an elderly black man. The other nurse had helped him move to a wheelchair nearby. I wondered at the timing.

I spoke to the nurse who had helped Bob: "Thank you, I'm so glad Bob can lie down, but we didn't mean to take a mattress from someone else. Wasn't that other man lying here?"

"It's okay," she said. "He wanted to move to the wheelchair." She placed a pillow under Bob's head. Then both nurses walked to the other end of the ramp, heading to the back of the garage.

I looked over at the other patient. He was a thin, slightly built man, sitting fairly straight in a wheelchair with foot rests, his hands in his lap, his gaze focused out the side of the garage. I walked over to him.

"Sir," I said. "I just want to make sure you're okay."

He looked up at me and nodded. "Okay."

"My husband needed to lie down and he's on that mattress you were on. The nurses said you wanted to move into the wheelchair. Is that right?"

"No," he said. "They ask me to move, so I did."

"But we didn't mean for them to move you if you didn't want to," I said.

"I understand how it is," he said. "Understand more than they think. Just do what they tell me."

I was silent, unsure what to do. I wanted Bob to lie flat, and I hated to have him go back to that wheelchair. But it wasn't right for us to take this man's mattress.

"We didn't intend to make you move," I said. "Do you want to move back? I'll get the nurses to help if you do."

He shook his head. "Okay here," he said, though his mouth had a slight grimace of annoyance. His burnished face and bald head were wrinkled, deep lines between nostrils and lips, furrows on the brow, and fine lines at the edge of his eyes—from pain or laughter, I couldn't tell.

"Well, let me know if you change your mind," I said. "Maybe we'll all get out of here before too much longer."

"Hope so," he said, one corner of his mouth curling up. "Don't seem to be much happening."

"You got that right," I said. "And nobody seems to know anything. You let me know if you need something, okay?" His look of annoyance had changed to a kind of resigned bemusement.

I walked back down the slope to Bob. He was lying in full sun now, but his eyes were closed and he looked much less distressed. The whole episode had troubled me, but both of them seemed to be okay for the time being. I decided to keep my eye on our mattress donor. He didn't have anyone with him, and I'd try to help him however I could.

The sun sank lower, and no more helicopters appeared although a few could be seen flying off in the distance, back and forth from other parts of the city. The patients around us by now were subdued, or maybe asleep. A kind of heated stupor had descended on Magnolia garage. The only sign of activity came from a number of men in scrubs who apparently were doctors. They had made several trips up and down from the helipad above us. One, bald and with the build of a runner, came down three times in the space of about thirty minutes, looking harried, each time asking a nurse near us for a head count of patients waiting in our group at one end of the garage. I recognized Joanne, the charge nurse from Clara Wing.

"Fourteen," she answered for the third time. He moved on, hardly hearing her answer. I caught her eye, and a knowing look passed between us as she said under her breath, "And fourteen the last two times you asked."

The doctors seemed to move in circles, endlessly conferring.

A few minutes later, the stocky "not in charge" doctor, hands still in her pockets, reappeared, looking ready to address our group again.

"Excuse me," I said, "But if you're not in charge, who is?"

"Dr. Deichmann," she said. I learned later that Dr. Richard Deichmann was Memorial/Baptist's Chief of Medicine. He was on the scene, among those leading the evacuation, though I don't know if he was one of the doctors I saw or talked to that day. A total of about twenty-five physicians were on duty in the days after the storm.

The not-in-charge doctor repeated her message that the staff were doing everything they could and we must be patient. Her tone was again condescending, as if she were admonishing a group of whining children.

Now I bristled. "Thank you," I said, "But we don't need a lecture—we need information. I don't mean to be difficult, but my husband and these other patients are tired, and we have been waiting *all day.*"

Her face changed, and I thought perhaps she suddenly saw the situation from the patients' point of view. Looking back, it seems more probable she was wondering why she had to put up with belligerent wives on top of everything else.

"I know," she said. "But I've been working since Saturday, most of the staff have been working since Saturday, and we're doing the best we can. We have almost no outside support and very little communication. We can't tell you when the rescuers will come because we don't know."

I was chastened. I knew the staff was working hard. Later, hearing about people stranded on their rooftops, waiting alone for multiple days and nights, or on highway bridges in the blazing sun, I realized some people suffered far more than we did. At the time, though, the waiting in the unrelenting heat, with no toilets, no information, and no sense of when we'd get out, on top of my underlying worry about Bob, made me increasingly desperate.

I would have been even more desperate had I known that the government had stopped all the private helicopters from flying. The airspace over New Orleans had been restricted and put under state and federal control, so the helicopters that came on Tuesday from the private Acadian Ambulance Service weren't able to return. Although everyone expected a fleet of federal helicopters to arrive on Wednesday, only a few came in the morning, and then the skies were cleared for hours to make way for Air Force One. After that, with no explanation, helicopter arrivals at Memorial stopped.

Finally, when another of the circling doctors passed by, the harried runner with the bald head, I took the chance to speak to him: "Doctor, do you realize how hard it is to sit here waiting for hours and be told nothing?"

He halted. Sympathy, and the sudden recognition that patients and their families needed to be talked to, showed in his eyes. "I'm sorry, but nothing is pretty much all we know," he said. "We'll try to give you information when we can."

I thanked him. The seeming disorganization and the lack of information had gotten to me, but I didn't want to be a troublemaker, and I told myself to be patient. The last thing the staff needed was complaining. I hoped my speaking up wouldn't put Bob at the end of the list for getting out. That chorus from *Beauty and the Beast* echoed in my head: *Just a little scared, Neither one prepared....*

Chapter Five

Fear Death by Water

Wednesday, August 31

As the afternoon deepened into early dusk, two doctors—one was the harried bald man I'd spoken to awhile ago, the other in wrinkled scrubs, wearing a limp baseball cap and sneakers—came up the ramp and around the corner, and the one with the cap addressed all of us waiting on the eighth level. He announced that we should all go back down to the second level of the garage. No more helicopters would be coming once it was dark. Some of us might be taken out by boat, and we had to go downstairs to be ready, just in case. A voice from the group asked where the boats would take people. The doctors replied they didn't know—an answer we were getting all too used to hearing.

I went over to Bob and roused him from his mattress. "They say we have to go back downstairs," I told him. "Let me help you back into the wheelchair and I'll wheel you down."

"Oh, no. Not that wheelchair again. Why are they moving us?"

"We might be getting out by boat, but no one knows. Same old story."

He was grumpy, but he moved. It was an effort for him to raise himself from the mattress to a sitting position, and he held onto my arm as he shakily got to his feet and into the wheelchair. Beads of perspiration dotted his forehead. I handed him the water bottle and helped him position his feet. He had to hold them up to keep them from dragging the ground.

I guided Bob's wheelchair over to the circular exit ramp and started down, holding on to keep the chair from gaining too much momentum down the steep incline. I looked back several times to check on the progress of our mattress donor. He was coming down behind us, pushed by a volunteer. All the patients and their straggling family members moved slowly down the six levels of the garage, passing the animals that were housed on the various floors, their barks, howls, squawks, and screeches following us in the musty heat. When we reached the second level, we joined other patients and family who had come from other parts of the garage and gathered in a group near the hole in the wall.

The doctor wearing the cap spoke to us again, telling us we were going to spend the night where we were. "The hospital is rank and filthy," he said, "with rancid air and no plumbing. I wouldn't go in there myself—it's not healthy. We'll make you comfortable here, and tomorrow we'll leave."

There was a murmur of surprise from the crowd. "What about the boats?" someone said.

"We're not sure if boats will be coming," the doctor said. "If they do, some of you can maybe leave. We'll have to wait and see."

The prospect of a night in the garage was daunting, but people seemed to take in the news and resign themselves, moving to get settled for more waiting. I scavenged and spotted an unused wheelchair over at one side near the corner. It had footrests, so I rolled it over and helped Bob transfer from his chair into the new one. The chair itself looked just as uncomfortable, but at least he'd have some support for his legs. I felt sorry for the patients who were here alone, without family members to give them the extra care the staff was too busy to provide. I walked over to check on our mattress donor. He was patiently parked in his wheelchair, waiting, and though he looked weary, he said he was okay.

About twenty minutes later, the bald runner gathered us for another announcement. One boat was coming, and any patients who could walk unassisted could board this boat if they wished. He warned that anyone going would have to be fully mobile: "You'll have to get into the boat without help, get out of the boat by yourself, and walk a short distance to a bus. No medical help will be there. Who wants to leave in this boat?"

About eight hands went up, and those people began preparing to leave. It was clear to me there was no way Bob could maneuver himself into a boat and make that trip, even with me to help him—and it didn't sound like they'd let me go. We would wait.

I didn't see the group leave, but the next day, I encountered one of them still in the garage, a tall man wearing a brown plaid bathrobe over his hospital gown. "Didn't you leave last night in a boat?" I asked.

"I tried," he said. "I'm here because of my heart. I didn't realize how much stamina would be needed to get in that boat. Couldn't handle it. Had to stay."

Meanwhile, more conferring was going on in the garage. Suddenly, the doctor wearing the cap raised his voice for another announcement.

"Okay, attention, everybody," he said. "We're not going to stay in the garage after all. For your own security, you're all going back into the hospital, back to your rooms."

I couldn't believe what I'd heard. Surely they wouldn't send us back into that hot, filthy hospital. How could they do that? The thought of it was too much. And whose security were they really thinking about? I'd rather take our chances in the garage than go back into that rank, dirty building. It would be unbearably hot, and by now the toilets would be overflowing—it couldn't be healthy. I waited until I could catch the doctor alone, just as he turned to leave.

"Doctor, please, why can't we stay here?" I pleaded.

"Security has decided the garage isn't safe," he said. "There are people roaming the streets with guns. They don't want you all out in the open here."

"But the garage is enclosed, at least partly. We're in a group, we're not out in the open. You yourself just said it's not healthy in the hospital. I don't want my husband to go back in there." The enclosed garage was beginning to feel like a cage, but at least the air was fresher than inside.

He was silent.

I repeated my plea: "Please don't make us go back in there—it's brutal. You've got to let us stay outside." I was calm but adamant. His face was expressionless, but he seemed to listen.

"Let me see," he said, and walked over to a group of other doctors and staff. More conferring. They were joined by a couple of people who were with patients. I hoped others felt the way I did and would convince them not to send us back into that building. I was preparing to be even more adamant, to argue logically, or to do what Southerners called "pitch a fit." I was *not* going to let them send Bob back into that hellish place.

Finally we got the announcement I'd hoped for: we would be spending the night in the garage after all, and staff would make us as comfortable as they could. Like a herd of weary, dirty, disgruntled sheep, the group on the second level of Magnolia garage had first settled down, then prepared to move, and now, amid minor grumbling and "why don't they make up their minds" comments, all of us turned once again to find a place where we could bed down for the night.

I wheeled Bob over to a spot behind two parked cars, across from the side of the garage where the open half-wall would give us a breeze if any breeze were to be had. The floor sloped up slightly as it approached the turn to the next level, but the brakes on the wheelchair held. It was barely dusk, but the interior of the garage was dark and musty, crowded with vehicles. Where light pierced the shadows, dust floated. The grey concrete ceiling seemed so low I could almost touch it, and the air reeked of rubber.

Soon nurses and volunteers began carrying in armfuls of mattresses, pallets, and pillows and they helped Bob and the other patients out of their wheelchairs and onto the mattresses, which put a couple of inches of padding between their bodies and the dirty concrete floor. Mattresses were spaced haphazardly from one end of the garage up the slope toward the next level. Once the patients were settled, pallets were given to the rest of us who wanted them. The pallets were thinner than the mattresses but at least gave us some padding to lie on. I stashed the empty wheelchair between the parked cars in case we'd need it later, and I laid my pallet next to Bob.

The words came back to me, but not the tune. "Bob, remember that old blues song, 'Make Me a Pallet on Your Floor'?" I said. "Do you remember how it goes?"

Music had always been important in our lives, and Bob's musical knowledge was extensive and eclectic. Though he hadn't played in years, he'd trained as a pianist and in college had played second piano for some of the gifted Texas musicians of his generation—he'd told me of accompanying Van Cliburn for some of his long-ago rehearsals. But after a year as a music major, Bob had decided he'd never be good enough to play concert piano, so he'd switched his field to comparative literature. He said his musical background gave him a special connection to language and the rhythms and nuances of literature. I played guitar years ago. We both had a deep love for all things musical, especially the blues and traditional jazz that filled the air of New Orleans.

"Sing?" he said. "After the day I've had and we're camped out in a garage, you want me to sing? Have you lost your mind?"

"I can't remember. It'll drive me crazy."

He shook his head, but then in his deep baritone, he softly hummed the tune. I joined in, and in a low voice, I sang the song, quietly in our spot between the cars:

> *Make me down a pallet on your floor*
> *Make it soft, make it low, make it close*
> > *behind the door,*
> *Make me down a pallet on your floor.*

I'd never imagined that song's scenario to be a parking garage.

Before settling down, I made a quick trip up the circular ramps to the seventh level to get a few things from our car to make us more comfortable, mainly the flashlight I'd brought to the hospital. Darkness would come soon, and I wanted that flashlight near us. Despite that doctor's reference to "people in the street with guns," I didn't really feel unsafe in the garage, and I hadn't heard any noises that sounded like gunfire. If anything, the spaces outside the hospital and garage seemed eerily quiet in the deepening dusk, but I knew it was going to get very dark once night came, and I was glad I'd brought the flashlight.

This was perhaps one time when lack of information was a help. Had I known about the anarchy and marauding being reported around us, I would have been terrified. Ignorant, I simply felt marooned, miserable but glad not to be inside the airless, stifling cesspit the hospital had become.

Later, I learned that as water inundated surrounding neighborhoods, desperate people came to the hospital for refuge. Already short on supplies and fearing looters, hospital officials told guards to keep outsiders from entering. A young woman from nearby Cadiz Street spent hours on the ramp by the ER, waiting with her four-year-old son and begging for help. Finally, she told a guard, "If my child drowns, it's going to be on your conscience." The guard let them in.

When I returned to the second level, nurses had set up tables in the center of the group, and volunteers were carrying in supplies. I recognized tall, calm LaShandra and auburn-haired Andrea from the oncology unit, both helping to position huge jugs of hand sanitizer, boxes of latex gloves, pads, dressings, bandages, and adult diapers on the central tables. A pharmacist came to talk to each patient, asking what medications were needed for the night and then going to fetch them. After many months, I knew exactly what drugs Bob was using and could rattle off the list of names and doses. I supposed the patients who didn't have family with them or who didn't know their medications had to rely on written records in their charts, still with them at that point. Soon the pharmacist returned with Bob's anti-nausea and pain pills and some antibiotic pills for me, since I wouldn't be able to fill the prescription I'd been given in the ER.

At least four flats of bottled water were stacked near the tables—so far, there seemed to be no shortage of water here. I learned later that the hospital's supply of water was dwindling alarmingly. Nurses kept reminding all of us to stay hydrated in the debilitating heat. A family member near me asked a doctor about toilets. His answer was that she could go back through the hole into the hospital if she wished, but the plumbing inside had shut down and all the toilets had stopped working. The alternative was to find somewhere out of the way in the garage.

When needed, nurses helped patients to use bedpans, or use adult diapers—where those would later be disposed of, I didn't like to speculate. Volunteers occasionally held up sheets to provide a semblance of privacy, but we were all packed so closely together real privacy wasn't possible. The waste from the humans and animals in the garage had to go somewhere, but it wasn't yet openly in evidence, although the humid air was taking on strong hints of sewer odors. So far, I hadn't felt the need for a toilet, and I hoped I could postpone that moment for as long as possible.

Dusk deepened, and murmured conversations occasionally broke the silence of the sweltering garage. At dinner time, two volunteers came around, the first offering packages of cheese and peanut butter crackers and the second carrying a box of small cans holding—of all things—Vienna sausages.

"Bob, guess what's for dinner?" I said as he lay on his pallet. "How about a Vienna sausage?"

"A what?" he said. "Good God. That's bizarre. I don't think so."

I settled for more crackers, and so did Bob. Vienna sausages were not exactly routine hospital fare—I wondered why the hospital even had a supply. Later I discovered they didn't. The cases of Vienna sausages were dropped by one of the few helicopters that landed earlier. Asked what they needed, hospital officials had asked for generators, oxygen, flashlights, batteries.

Instead, they got Vienna sausages.

Glumly, I contemplated my package of crackers, six garish orange squares with a thin layer of brown processed cheese between the squares. They were less than appealing, but I supposed we should try to eat them. There was no knowing when we'd get anything better. I opened

Bob's for him, and he managed to eat just one. Then I opened my own package.

The crackers were as powdery as they looked. The heat was stultifying. It had been almost this hot that October day nearly a year ago when we left Houston, the six-hour drive back to New Orleans ahead of us. We'd made the same drive twice before, but this time we faced it without the dread of more drugs, more pain, more sickness at the destination. Bob had finished his third course of chemo and afterward had endured two days of tests: CAT scan, bone scan, MRI, blood analysis, the whole shebang. After tense days of waiting, the M. D. Anderson doctor had given us the best possible news: all the tests were clear. The chemo had worked. No sign of cancer cells anywhere in Bob's body remained. The relief I felt was like a warm wave washing over me, draining muscles of tension and mind of worry.

It was over. We were free.

We packed the car and headed east on Interstate 10, feeling like parolees released from prison. We drove to the beat of Wynton Marsalis's trumpet and Dr. Michael White's clarinet, glad to be leaving Houston in the rear view mirror, enjoying the early fall scenery, making plans for the upcoming holidays. On an impulse, we decided to stop overnight in Lafayette, just because we could. We had no schedule, no appointments at doctors' offices or hospitals, no one to answer to but ourselves. We'd make it a leisurely evening, a celebration.

"Oysters," said Bob. "That's what I want—a huge tray of ice-cold oysters."

We knew where to go. We'd discovered the seafood restaurant on a previous trip, just down the road from the Courtyard Inn where we stayed. That would be our first stop, then we'd make it a traveling meal—we'd go further down the highway for some Cajun music.

The waitress put the two trays in front of us, large circles of shaved white ice surrounding twelve grey, glistening oysters nestled in their half-shells. Bob hadn't dared eat raw oysters during his treatments, fearing their effect on his compromised immune system. I had abstained out of solidarity. We took our time mixing the sauce, dropping a dollop of white horseradish into the small bowl of tomato sauce and swirling it around, adding drops of Tabasco—just a few for me, but Bob liked his hot. After dribbling juice from lemon wedges, we each speared a plump oyster on our fork, dipped it in the sauce, then lifted it high. Forks poised between tray and mouth, we looked at each other and smiled.

"Here's to us, to the future," I said.

"Cheers," said Bob.

That first taste was a blast of cold, and the slick texture and subtle flavor of the oyster blended with the hotness of the sauce. Heaven. We savored every one, in between sips of icy Abita Amber from frosted schooners.

Afterward, we drove down the road for a second course. At a Cajun dance hall cum restaurant, we sat at an old cypress table heaped with several pounds of fiery red crawfish, boiled to perfection with all the sides: round white new potatoes, small cobs of yellow corn, French bread. Neither of us had totally mastered the technique of eating crawfish, but with instruction from friends who were native New Orleanians and lots of practice, we were making progress. Freeing the tail meat from the thick red shells took us twice as long as it did the people around us, but tonight we had all the time in the world. We peeled and ate, laughing at our lack of skill, enjoying the band playing familiar Cajun tunes. The large restaurant was full of people of all ages, from toddlers to courting couples to grizzled grandparents, all gathered around tables heaped with crawfish and mounds of fried catfish, shrimp, and oysters.

Couples of all ages moved on the dance floor, all doing an almost choreographed two-step in a slow-moving circle, counter-clockwise, swaying to the sounds of the accordion, fiddles, and guitars. Lights flickered in the background. Some faces were alight with smiles. Others were placid, expressionless, slowly circling the crowded floor. Small children danced with each other, doing studied, elaborate versions of the two-step, mimicking their elders.

"We could be sitting here a hundred years ago and I bet the scene would be the same," Bob said.

"At the rate we're peeling these crawfish, we might be here for another hundred years," I said.

"I'm glad we're here now," said Bob. "Here's to more years of music, more years of oysters, and as much time as it takes to conquer crawfish."

We raised and touched our frosty glasses of ale, a smiling toast to our future.

That vision of the future certainly hadn't included being marooned in Magnolia Garage.

Just before dark, Bill Quigley, the monk-haired attorney who had helped on my trip to stow our stuff, rushed up the ramp followed by another volunteer. They carried a bed sheet they'd made into a large sign. Holding it up, they told the assembled family members that helicopters and boats had stopped coming, and it angered them to see boats that could be used to evacuate people pass by carrying only photographers. They'd written large black letters on the white sheet: "Help—people are dying." Many of us voiced our support and applauded as they walked calmly but determinedly toward the roof, where they intended to hang the banner over the side of the building and try to attract attention. Later, I realized that the photographers and videographers were the ones who informed those outside the city of our plight, and without them, rescue operations at Memorial and all over the city might have been delayed even longer than they were. Still, it was a fine line, and watching them sail by in boats, taking pictures while we all remained trapped, was hard.

Before long, we heard the sound of choppers in the distance, but they didn't come close. I locked eyes with a young woman sitting near me, next to her frail father, still in a wheelchair.

"They coming but they not stopping," she said ruefully.

"Must be just trying to give us a thrill," I said with a smile.

"Huh," she said. "You right." She rolled her eyes and shook her head.

I was tired and worried, but I don't remember feeling totally desperate yet. It still seemed probable we would get out, eventually. It's a tribute to Memorial's staff that they didn't communicate their rising fears to the patients. Later, I learned how chaotic the whole rescue operation had been. Hospital officials were unable to talk to police or other government authorities, and communication with Tenet headquarters was sporadic. Against all reason, National Guardsmen and state police had forced the doctors to close the ramp by the ER hours before dark, stopping boats from docking there and taking people out. Defying that order, hospital staff had established a clandestine dock on a ramp at the other side of the garage and managed to load a few more boats before darkness fell, but no one had any information about when, or whether, more boats or helicopters would arrive or if they did, where they would take evacuees. Overall in the flooded city, and in our little part of it, there seemed to be no information, no coordination, no plan. I learned later that the rumors of violence had some authorities, especially people from outside the city, making decisions based on rumor and fear. The reports of looters running rampant took on racial overtones, and some rescue groups from other areas were afraid to enter the city. Others were turned back, forbidden to continue their rescue missions by FEMA or other authorities. Not only were all of us stranded citizens kept from getting out—their decisions meant needed supplies couldn't get in.

Meanwhile, our motley group settled down for a Magnolia night. Nurses moved from the central table back and forth to patients, and now I recognized Nurse Carolyn among them. She came over to greet us, and it was good to see her familiar face. She worked with a team of other nurses, helping with bedpans and pads, changing dressings, giving medications, making sure everybody had water, trying to keep patients safe and calm. We had everything we needed except toilets, comfort, and escape.

Before lying down to try to sleep, I walked over to the side of the garage and looked out. The city looked unreal—as far as I could see, everything was dark, with only a few lights scattered amid the blackness and quiet. I guessed those distant lights were from emergency generators, but they might also have been flashlights of people stranded on roofs. The far-off lights reflected on water, everywhere water. Later I learned that Memorial/Baptist sat almost dead center in the "bowl" of New Orleans, in between Lake Pontchartrain and the Mississippi, and when the levees collapsed, water drained straight toward the hospital. Outside, the scene took on an eerie beauty as moonlight glimmered on the deep water all around us.

Inside the garage, people slowly quieted. The howls of dogs caged all around and above us echoed on the humid air. Occasionally, someone strolled through our "camp" with a dog on a leash.

"Out for the evening walkies," Bob said when a middle-aged blonde woman in halter and shorts came through, leashed to a determined Yorkshire terrier.

"Unbelievable," I said. "It's like we're locked in a scene from *M.A.S.H.*"

"Too bad Hawkeye Pierce isn't coming to the rescue," said Bob.

The muggy air hung heavy in the dark garage, overlaid with the smells of oil and dirt and sweaty bodies. Bob finally closed his eyes and fell into a restless sleep, and I lay on the pallet near him and tried to do the same. I dozed for awhile but all of a sudden was jolted awake by the strong smell of urine. A male patient up the slope from me was sending a stream down the floor, and it was flowing inches from my head. I did the only thing I could: moved my pallet out of the path of the flow and tried to go back to sleep.

The thick and stifling heat of the day lingered in the dark garage. The combination of heat and humidity was suffocating, like breathing underwater. Several times I awoke to find a nurse or a young volunteer standing above Bob, fanning him with a large piece of cardboard. Some of the relatives of staff—teenagers and even younger—were helping out however they could. The blast of breeze lasted about five minutes, then the fanner moved on to another patient. The edge of the breeze hit me and felt wonderfully refreshing in the hot, sticky night. I drifted back to sleep.

Noise woke me sometime deep in the night. About five feet down the concrete slope from my pallet, I could see in the moonlight the top of someone's head, a dark bony skull with tight tufts of steel-gray hair poking out. The body lay on a mattress covered with a pale yellow sheet. Suddenly, the head jerked upward, the sheet flew off, and the skinny old woman sat up, talking in a loud voice. "Got to get up out of here. Lillyann coming to get me. Uh-huh. Get me home."

Pale arms reached out to grasp her shoulders, and the low voice of a nurse in green scrubs said, "Here, now, it's okay, you just lie back. Hush now, take it easy, just relax."

But the woman I'll call Ms. Johnson shrugged, moving a bony shoulder out of the nurse's grasp. "No, no, got to be going. Lillyann coming." The soiled and wrinkled hospital gown hung loosely on her fragile frame, one side falling off a shoulder and down one dusky arm.

"Who is Lillyann?" asked the nurse. "Tell me about her. Is she here with you?"

"She at home. Storm coming, she bring me here. Let me up."

"No, Ms. Johnson, you need to stay here," said the nurse. "We'll be leaving soon, but right now you need to be quiet. People are sleeping. Just be still. You're going to feel better soon."

The nurse tried to ease the woman back onto the mattress, but she kept resisting, her arms flailing and her head moving from side to side. "Come on, Ms. Johnson, lie back and I'll fan you so you'll feel cooler. Be quiet, now. Here's some water. I'll hold this bottle and you take a sip of water."

The woman put her lips to the bottle for a minute then pushed it away. "No, baby, let me up. It too hot. Need to get home. Burning up. Head hurts. Too many peoples here. Can't breathe. Make my groceries. Where my dress?" With one hand, she ripped open the snaps on one shoulder, and her gown fell open, exposing her bony chest, pendulous breasts hanging loosely above her thin waist.

"No, Ms. Johnson, put this back on now." The nurse tried to hold the woman steady and cover her. "You got to cover up. There's people here all around you. That's right, put your arm back in this gown. Here, I'll snap you up. Now you relax and lie down."

The woman kept babbling as the nurse, with one hand, gently pushed her flat onto the mattress. With her other hand, the nurse fanned a piece of cardboard back and forth, causing the tight tufts of grey hair to flutter in the breeze. Somewhere below us, a dog barked insistently, short, high yaps carried on the stifling night air. For awhile, the old woman was quiet while the nurse moved the cardboard over her, back and forth. I was just dozing off when suddenly the old lady jerked upright again, this time almost making it to her feet, one thin leg shaking.

"I need some stamps!" she bellowed.

Several nurses rushed over to quiet her, helping her to lie back on her pallet, laughing quietly among themselves. At the same time, a new sound, a dull roar, echoed from somewhere above us, and two large metal fans standing at each end of the patient enclave started whirring. The roar was from a small generator that had been moved onto the third level of the garage. I wondered what was powering the generator and thought it was probably gas siphoned from cars above us. Wherever they came from, the fans were a godsend in the steamy garage.

The nurses seemed to be rotating in shifts, some catching a few minutes of sleep on pallets around us when they could, others attending to the rest of us. They were unfailingly cheerful, trying quietly to reassure us although they didn't seem to have any more information than we did. I realized again how hard they'd been working, and for how long—many, like Carolyn, had been on duty for more than four days straight, with only brief breaks. I hoped these dedicated employees would somehow be rewarded, by the city, the state, and Tenet Healthcare, for their heroic work.

Later, I learned that many were laid off. Others were arrested for murder.

Sometime in the early morning darkness, I awoke and couldn't get back to sleep. I took a turn fanning Bob for awhile. Then, worried and restless, I decided I should go back into the hospital and get the bags I left there, especially the syringes full of Bob's expensive medication. Maybe that drug, called Lovenox, wouldn't be available where he was going, and we should send the syringes along with him. Nurse Carolyn was working at the central table, and I walked over to her.

"I need to go back inside," I said. "I want to get that stuff I left on the third floor."

"You absolutely can't go back in that hospital," Carolyn said. "There are people roaming around with guns in there. It's not safe." I wasn't sure who she was talking about. I heard later that there were rumors of looters in the neighborhood, that a Rite Aid drug store a block away was entered and emptied. I read reports much later that some nurses heard gun shots near the hospital and were afraid looters would break in looking for drugs. But no one ever offered evidence of any acts of violence within Memorial Hospital itself during those dark days. On the contrary, all I saw were acts of kindness and compassion, from staff, volunteers, family members, and eventually from people who came to our rescue. Maybe the "people with guns" Carolyn was referring to were the security guards.

I persisted, pleading that Bob's medicine was there and he needed those syringes. She took a deep breath, gave me an annoyed look, and I was sure she was about to forbid me again. Instead, she walked over to two tall black men standing at the side of the garage. They both had on khaki shorts with gun belts strapped at their waists. As she talked to them, they looked over at me and nodded. Then they followed Carolyn over to where I waited.

"These guards are going to escort you," she said. "You can't go in there alone."

"Okay, wonderful." I looked at the men. "Thank you, I'm grateful."

I glanced at Bob and saw his eyes were open. "I'm going back to the room to get some of the stuff I left," I told him. "I won't be gone long." He was still half-asleep, and I left before he could protest.

The two guards were holding flashlights. I grabbed mine, and we set off, past the dark stairs where I'd fallen yesterday. They climbed through the hole in the wall, then one turned and offered his hand and I followed. Emerging from the hole into the dark interior of the hospital, I felt like Alice in a strange land. The large lobby was full of people, alone and in groups, sleeping, awake, crowded on furniture and floors in the darkness. The air was thick and sweltering and smelled foul. We passed by the chapel, where I'd gone a few times for quiet moments alone during Bob's earlier stays at Memorial. I didn't know it, but that chapel was now full of dead bodies, corpses of patients who had died in the days since the storm. The hospital's morgue was in the flooded basement, so bodies were being taken to the tiny chapel on the second level and stacked under the stained glass. There were no more body bags, so the dead were wrapped in sheets. The stack of corpses was growing daily—the final tally would reach thirty-four. The message on Bill Quigley's banner was literally true—people were dying.

I followed the guards up the dark stairwell to the third floor, glad I wasn't alone. This floor was pitch black, hot, deserted, and a mess. The beams from our flashlights cast cones of pale light. We walked past a large vending machine pushed onto its side, the glass on the front smashed, the innards missing. The carpeted floor was covered with abandoned garbage, trash, and mounds of refuse, strewn helter skelter. We walked down the hallway toward the empty patients' rooms.

"What number that room?" one of the guards asked me.

"We were in 3158 and my stuff's in a staff room close by."

We opened doors, shining light inside, and finally opened the right one. Jubilant, I spotted my canvas tote, my file box, and a plastic sack that I thought must be Nurse Carolyn's. I debated taking it all but decided to take only the canvas tote, thinking it contained the syringes along with other medicines and the notebook containing Bob's medical records. Later, I discovered I'd left the expensive syringes behind after all, in the plastic sack I thought was Carolyn's. Why I had been so focused on those syringes is beyond me now. It probably wouldn't have been safe to use them anyway, since they'd been stewing in one-hundred-plus-degree heat for two days.

Triumphant, I followed the guards as we made our way back through the dark, deserted hallways. I was grateful they were with me, and armed, though we didn't encounter anyone threatening. Still, the signs of upheaval, the silence, and the trash strewn everywhere, as if people had run amok through the hallways, created an ominous atmosphere. When we got back to the garage, I thanked the guards heartily. I don't think they were part of Memorial's regular security staff. I learned later that security guards, police and National Guardsmen who had been at the hospital left on boats earlier that day, either for other missions or simply to get themselves out, so doctors deputized members of the maintenance staff and gave them guns. Whoever these two were, I was grateful to them for indulging my obsessive quest.

Leaving the enclave on the second level one more time, I made a final trip up the ramp to our car, to stash what I couldn't take with me. I also adjusted the packet I would stuff in my waistband. In the packet and my purse, I would carry cell phone, money, credit cards, drivers' licenses, the memory stick from my digital camera, car registration, insurance and tax papers, and our parking permit for the French Quarter—a document worth gold in times past. I didn't stop to think that post-Katrina it would likely be useless. In the canvas tote, I'd carry our various medications, supplies, and the notebook with all Bob's medical records. The nurses had convinced me not to try to take the laptop, so I left that locked in the trunk with everything else. When I'd asked the guards about security after the evacuation, they told me that once everybody was out, there would be no more security. The hospital and garage would be abandoned and open, so chances were good that everything in the car would be stolen, maybe even the car itself.

I have no choice, I thought. I'll have to hope for the best. What matters is for us to get out.

When I got back to the second level, dawn was near. A band of lavender light had appeared on the horizon, and wispy clouds floated and gathered in the sky. Bob and I had long loved the works of Tennessee Williams—I suspect they were part of the reason we'd fallen in love with New Orleans. So much of what Tennessee loved about New Orleans we loved, too. In the last decade of his career Bob had taught a seminar on Tennessee's plays and films. Walking in the Quarter, Bob often remarked on what Tennessee had written once in a letter about the light being different in New Orleans, how "the clouds and the sky seem so close...that you could touch them....fleecy and in continual motion." Even now, as New Orleans was sinking underwater, the city's sky moved close overhead, with a quiet and shifting beauty.

People began to stir. Bob soon woke up, and we speculated about the day ahead. A group of nurses near us were talking about where they'd go. Most of them seemed to believe their homes were flooded and their jobs at this hospital were probably over. Some talked about leaving New Orleans for good, going to other hospitals in the Tenet system elsewhere in Louisiana. Carolyn assured me she'd take care of our file box, and once we were back in the city, I could call her and retrieve it. When I thanked her again, she talked about keeping things in perspective.

"Hey," she said, "this is just a storm and a flood. When I see your husband and these other patients, who are really sick or full of cancer, I'm thankful for my health. We'll get through this."

That "full of cancer" phrase stabbed me with fear, but I told myself that once we were out of here and back to chemo treatments, Bob would continue to beat back the disease.

After the first three rounds of chemo had worked and the cancer went into remission, our reprieve had been short. A sudden fever shocked us in mid-January, 2005. Doctors had forbidden Bob to get his usual flu shot because of the chemo, so we told each other he'd caught a flu, and Dr. Veith prescribed anti-flu medication. But the fever kept climbing, and for one long winter night I'd lain awake holding him as he shook with chills, keeping cool washcloths on his hot forehead until the fever finally broke near dawn. The next day, Bob felt well enough to get out of bed. Then, as he sat at the computer checking his email, he was suddenly racked with a new, powerful chill.

Frightened, I helped him back to bed, shaking, and called 911. Bob ended up back in Memorial for ten days, fighting another dangerous infection. He won that battle, but now fear hovered in the background of our days.

The onset of jaundice in April sent us back to M. D. Anderson, where the verdict was cruel indeed: the cancer was back and was spreading. Doctors offered some hope in a different chemotherapy, so Bob began another round of drugs, these more toxic and harsh. Nurses called one drug the "red devil." After six weeks, he wanted to be home: "I refuse to molder in this hospital any longer," he announced.

So we returned to New Orleans, hoping the city would work its magic on Bob's battered body and battle-weary psyche. We knew the cancer was active, but we were determined to keep fighting. Dr. Veith started Bob on another cycle of chemo in late July. Our goal was remission, and time—we hung on to the hope that the new drugs would stop the invader. Once, on a shuttle bus to the M. D. Anderson clinic, Bob had overheard a patient say he was back for annual tests.

"That's the place I'm hoping to get to," Bob told me. "Back every year for tests. That sounds good."

All along, despite some down times, we had both stayed hopeful, believing all we'd been told about the power of that positive attitude.

Now one final hurdle remained for me in the garage. All night long I had avoided having to use a bedpan, but now it was either that or squat somewhere behind a car. I hated to be a bother to the nurses, but I mentioned my need to one of them, and she said cheerfully, "No problem, come with me."

She moved a wheelchair over to the side of a parked car, put a bedpan in the seat, and she and another nurse held up a blanket to give me privacy. Alas, just as I was finishing, the bedpan slipped and my underpants got soaked.

"If I were you," said the nurse, "I'd lose those."

So I did.

Chapter Six

Hurry Up Please, It's Time

Thursday, September 1

By 6:30 a.m. nearly everyone around us was awake and beginning to gather belongings scattered around them on the garage floor. Muted conversations hummed with anticipation. Would help finally come? Would today be the day we'd finally get out? The water outside still surrounded us, lapping at the walls of the garage and glinting in the morning light. There was a slight early morning relief from the heat, but the humidity remained and we knew the garage would swelter again as the day wore on. I helped Bob into the wheelchair so he would be ready for the trip back up the ramp to the holding area for the helipad. I looked around for the mattress man, but I didn't see him. Perhaps he'd been one of the group who left in a boat last night.

As we gathered near the supply tables, nurses handed everyone a small box of dry cereal—Cheerios, mainly—and urged us all to eat, saying we'd need strength in the coming day. We had become a familiar group, and many of us chatted quietly, sharing our stories and trying to reassure one another. I overheard two nurses talking about patients on ventilators who were having to be ventilated by hand-compressed breathing bags, but no one in our group seemed to need a ventilator. Several did have tubes running from their noses to large oxygen tanks. One sixty-ish woman, who said she was in pain from recent knee surgery, told me she had come to Memorial to be with her granddaughter, who was a nurse. Now she was going to have to leave her granddaughter behind, and her two small dogs as well.

"They've had a good life," she said sadly. "I hate to leave them, but I can't take them. I hope somebody stops by the hospital after we're all gone and feeds them."

"Surely someone will," I said. In truth, I doubted it. I didn't like to think of what would happen to all the pets in the garage when their human caretakers finally left. Based on the response of rescuers so far, I didn't have high hopes that the animals would be saved before they starved.

Suddenly a young woman wearing a hospital gown and sitting quietly in a wheelchair started to shake violently. Her eyes rolled backward. Alarmed, nurses rushed to the supply table, and Joanne, the charge nurse, brought back a small carton of orange juice. The patient was having a diabetic seizure, and the juice solved the problem. She looked worn out and frail, but she stopped shaking and smiled weakly. What would they do once the supplies ran out and there was no more juice?

The sun rose higher. Nurses gathered all the patients in a circle and told us they were going to do a triage. Each patient had a paper tag pinned to his or her gown: those who could walk were marked with a "1" and those who needed help were given a "2." Bob got a "2." It seemed a very organized and efficient system. Yet later, when the evacuation actually began, I saw no evidence that anyone paid any attention whatsoever to those tags.

After awhile, movement around us seemed to increase, with people appearing from above to talk with nurses. All of us who could walk were ordered to start at once up the spiral ramp to level eight. I gave Bob a quick hug and told him I hoped I'd see him at the top, and then I started walking, constantly glancing behind me. I was relieved to see nurses begin to push Bob's and others' wheelchairs slowly up the ramp. When I got to the fifth level, the ER doctor with the sweatband and the ER nurse named Erin were standing near the side of the garage with their Irish setter between them. My eye still had the bandage on it, and they recognized me.

"How's the eye?" the doctor said.

"Okay—getting colorful, I think." I smiled.

"How's your husband doing?" Erin asked.

"So-so. He's had a rough couple of days. Looks like we might finally get out," I said, "not together, though."

Their faces both frowned with concern. "I hope y'all find each other soon," she said. "I wish your husband well."

"Thanks," I said. "Good luck to you, too, and thank you both for your help."

I kept walking, and as I rounded the curve up to the seventh level, suddenly the doctor I'd been short with yesterday, the not-in-charge woman with the school-marmish tone, rose up from where she'd obviously been squatting behind a parked car. We smiled sheepishly at each other.

"Hi," I said. "I want to apologize if I sounded harsh yesterday. I was frustrated. I hope you understand."

"I do," she said. "The problem was no one knew anything. Still don't."

"Well, good luck," I said, and kept walking. She turned, adjusting her clothing.

I'd given Bob my socks so he wouldn't have to travel in bare feet, so I had only sneakers on my feet. I was wearing a pair of cotton Capri slacks, and because of the bedpan accident, no underpants. The packet I'd stashed inside my waistband kept sliding down with each step, and I had to keep stopping to hike it up. Finally I decided it wasn't going to work—that packet wasn't going to stay in my waistband. Instead, I'd have to strap my purse around me and carry the small plastic sack in one hand and the canvas tote in the other. Surely that wasn't too much to carry onto a helicopter.

I got to the eighth level and stopped. The bedraggled group of patients and family slowly gathered again where we'd waited all day yesterday. Outside the hospital, all was quiet. The deep water looked murkier, and the sun glinted on the rainbow colors of oil slicks floating on the water's surface. Houses in the neighborhood looked forlorn, with water climbing up their walls. Boards and tree branches floated in the churning water, knocking against the roofs of cars submerged in the streets. The early-morning air in the garage smelled musty.

I met Bob's wheelchair as the nurse pushed him up the ramp, and I wheeled him to the side of the garage, the same spot where we'd waited before. Now it was three days after the storm. Would we finally get out? Everyone seemed to think helicopters would come today. I hoped they were right.

I realized all of a sudden that I hadn't seen any children today or yesterday. Where were the little ones who'd been sheltering in the hospital? What had become of the little pig-tailed girl playing *Beauty and the Beast*? They might still be with the crowds stranded inside the hellish hospital building, though I hoped somehow they had gotten out. The memory caused a reprise of those much-repeated lyrics: *Just a little change....*

Bob looked at me with one of his wry smiles. "Your eye looks like a purple sunset."

"I know," I said. "I can see people staring when they look at me. Maybe it'll get us sympathy and get us out."

"Hurry up please, it's time," said Bob.

"That's for sure," I said. The *Waste Land* references were seeming more and more fitting. I rested my hand on Bob's. He seemed paler today. The waiting had been hard on him. I handed him a bottle of water and urged him to take at least a sip.

We watched as patients were moved up to the end of the ramp. From there, they were put on sheet slings or backboards and carried up three flights of rusty metal stairs, steep as a fire escape. It took at least six people to carry each patient up, three on each side, sometimes more, and it looked like sweaty, back-breaking work. In fact, looking at those stairs, I would never have believed anyone could be carried up, yet I watched it happen. A few ambulatory patients or family members straggled up behind them. The morning sun blazed down, and the garage began to swelter again.

Would they manage to carry Bob safely up those scary-looking steps? Could I climb them myself? I had never liked carrying things on stairs since our Greek island-hopping experience years ago. The harbor at Mykonos was too small for our ferry to land, so they told us we'd have to disembark down a steep gangway on the outside of the ship, into a small motor boat bobbing on the water below.

"How will we do that with the luggage?" I asked Bob frantically.

"They'll help us," he said, and went in search of a crew member to ask about our bags.

Later, I wished we had a movie of our arrival on Mykonos—it could well have featured in an episode of *The Three Stooges* or a sitcom like *I Love Lucy*. Wearing a sun dress and sandals and clutching my purse and a small bag, I inched my way down the metal steps, trying to keep my skirt from blowing up around my head and trying to ignore the deep water far below me. Bob looked down anxiously from above, shouting encouragement and reminding me to hang on, as if my white-knuckled hands weren't clamped on the railings for dear life.

Finally I reached the bottom and was helped into the tiny motorboat by a smiling Greek sailor. I held my breath as Bob made his way slowly down the steep steps, trying to carry one of our large suitcases. It was too unwieldy, and he had to hand the bag back up to the crew on deck, leave it and descend alone. Finally he dropped into the boat beside me, sweating. After that, the ferry crew attached our suitcases to ropes and sent them down one by one, lowering them into the boat. With the two large bags propped bow and stern and the other luggage arranged around us, I feared we might sink before we ever made the harbor, but the small boat chugged slowly in and deposited us on the dock, shaky but with luggage intact. At least I'd be going up these heliport steps, rather than down —going up might be easier.

The familiar *thwack thwacks* sounded overhead, and one by one, helicopters started landing. At last, I thought. Maybe today we'd really get out. As each helicopter took off, more patients were taken up, and the rest of us turned away from the blasts of gritty air the 'copters blew in their wake. The helicopters leaving seemed to head upriver, toward the west.

Soon the patient who had had the insulin crisis earlier was carried on a backboard jerkily up the metal stairs. Then I saw a nurse approach the dark-haired man

I'd talked to yesterday about his uncle. She spoke to him, and he started walking up the ramp toward the stairs. The nurse came over to me.

"We need another person who can walk," she said. She looked at my vinyl hospital bracelet. "You're a patient, aren't you?"

"My husband's a patient, and I'm waiting with him," I said, "but I was in the ER Tuesday night."

"I thought so. You're the Code Sprint. Come with me."

"I'd rather wait with my husband—couldn't we go together?" I knew what her answer would be, but I made one final try anyway.

She shook her head. "No, you've got to come now."

I bent down to give Bob a hug. "Don't worry," I said. "Wherever they take us, I'll find you as soon as I can."

He smiled wanly. "Okay. I love you. Be careful." A deep furrow creased his brow, and his eyes looked fearful. I bent for another quick hug.

I followed the nurse toward the roof and up the steep metal stairs. Halfway, she turned and took the canvas tote so I could hold on to the railing. At the top, we walked about twenty yards over the roof toward another set of stairs, with a short flight down, then another up to the next level of the roof. I had to stop and catch my breath.

"Come on, you're doing fine," said the nurse.

I suddenly felt near tears. "I'm so afraid I won't be able to find my husband."

"Don't worry," she said. "We'll have you together again soon, I promise."

After the past three days, I didn't have much confidence that she could fulfill that promise. I kept walking.

The roof was flat, with open sides, and it seemed incredibly high. I focused my eyes straight ahead and tried not to look over the edge. Not far from the top of the stairs, we entered a kind of raised catwalk tunnel, covered with Plexiglas and leading to the helipad. The tunnel was full of people, sprawled on the ground or sitting against the walls, and we had to make our way over a path strewn with empty water bottles, discarded boxes and bags, and other trash. The nurse pushed me toward the helipad. When I turned to take my canvas tote, she held it back, and someone else grabbed the plastic sack out of my hands.

"My husband's medicine is in there," I protested as I reached for the tote.

"He's going to a hospital, he'll get medicine there."

I hesitated, but she pushed me toward the waiting chopper. "Go! Go now, or you may not get out at all."

With that, I ran toward the orange helicopter, stooping to avoid its whirring blades. A woman in denim shorts and a sun visor waited to help me climb through its open side. I was the third passenger—the diabetic patient and the walking nephew were the other two—and we all sat on the floor directly behind the pilot and co-pilot, who wore flight uniforms and aviator helmets. There seemed to be room, so I told the co-pilot I'd left my canvas tote, emphasizing that it held medical records. He yelled to someone on the ground, and suddenly my tote was pushed into my arms. I was glad to have it but worried that all our financial papers were in the plastic packet, and I felt extremely distressed to leave it behind. I was losing the bag, Bob, and all control over our lives.

The blades whirred faster, and now the pilot prepared for take-off. The co-pilot turned around to check on the three of us. Still hungry for information, I asked him if he could tell us where we were going. He shook his head to say no and adjusted his headphones as the helicopter lifted slowly off the ground. Its sides were open, with no doors, and as we cleared the edge of the helipad, looking down I could see Bob sitting alone in his wheelchair, gazing up.

I waved.

As we rose, he looked smaller and smaller.

We flew low, toward the west, over Uptown and Carrollton toward neighboring Jefferson Parish. Everywhere I looked, I saw water. I couldn't identify streets or landmarks. Water engulfed streets and houses. The tops of huge trees stretched above absurdly short trunks, their bottom halves submerged. Cars that had been parked on neutral grounds to keep them dry instead were underwater. The ride was an overall impression of water, everywhere it didn't belong. A city drowning.

Before long, the pilot's headphones crackled with some type of instructions, and we started a circular descent toward what looked like New Orleans' Louis Armstrong Airport. As we landed, I recognized the terminal buildings and runways. The nephew and I were helped to climb down, and we ducked under the whirring blades. Two men jumped into the 'copter and helped the diabetic patient out of the aircraft and into a waiting wheelchair, and we followed as she was wheeled toward the terminal. I looked behind us. Our helicopter was already rising from the tarmac, taking off for another rescue.

I learned later that the Coast Guard had been flying for two days—except, of course, when the skies had to be cleared for hours so Air Force One could give the President his sightseeing tour—but many of the Coast Guard helicopters were busy lifting people off rooftops. Doctors at Memorial had been told Thursday morning that no help was coming and "you're on your own." As conditions at Memorial got more desperate, with no hope of assistance from federal or state government agencies, Tenet was trying to hire a fleet of helicopters to evacuate Memorial's patients, family, and eventually staff. Those helicopters began to land later in the day on Thursday, but before they did, a group of Coast Guard helicopters showed up unexpectedly and flew several loads of people out of Magnolia garage. At the time, I had no idea whose helicopter I was on—all I knew was I was leaving the hospital, and leaving Bob.

We entered an open door into the airport's lower passenger level, a huge space with baggage carousels and a few seating areas. The room was sparsely populated: a few people on stretchers lay on the floor at one side, and people in wheelchairs were lined up near the side of the doors. An emergency worker with some sort of badge told those of us walking to keep going up the stairs at the far end.

"I want to wait for my husband," I said. "He's a hospital patient. He'll be coming in a helicopter behind me."

"Well, okay," he said. "Wait down here. Once you go up those stairs, no coming back down."

I took out my cell phone and tried it, but I got no signal. On a wall at the far side of the room, I spied a bank of pay phones, and I walked over to see if by chance those would work, but they were dead.

I knew our family would be trying to locate both of us, and I was right. The emails among my brother, sisters, and Bob's nephews and their wives had begun on Tuesday when they learned of the evacuation from my frantic calls. Their messages continued on Wednesday and intensified on Thursday. At 3:45 a.m. on Thursday, my brother was awake at his home in Raleigh, and his email to other family members reflects his growing concern:

> Lost touch with Carolyn and Bob in New Orleans sometime Tuesday afternoon. Evacuation was planned from Memorial next day....I was worried but relatively OK yesterday but now very worried. It seems like they fell off the earth, and I am especially worried that they were separated and Carolyn is mingled with tens of thousands of people somewhere with no way to communicate with Bob or us, and that Bob may be doing poorly.

Our relatives were working the phones, trying to find some official information about where evacuees were being taken. They were unable to learn anything definite. My brother wrote that he had "called all major Baton Rouge hospitals; no record of Bob admitted. Tried some in Houston, ditto. Getting through to New Orleans impossible since yesterday. Baton Rouge emergency numbers also swamped." My sister Lorraine called other hospitals in Houston, and her hopes rose when she found a patient named Robert Perry in one of them. But when she asked hospital officials to find out if this patient was evacuated from Memorial/Baptist Hospital in New Orleans and had a wife named Carolyn, the answer was no—it was the wrong Robert Perry.

Knowing that Tenet Healthcare was the owner of Memorial and thus responsible for its patients, they tried calling Tenet for information. My sister Liz got through, but her email sent on Thursday at 8:27 a.m. shows the confusion and misinformation she encountered at Tenet:

> I got thru to Tenet HQ Media Relations (Val) who said she thought most of the patients were out now and they were evacuating staff today. They hired a fleet of private helicopters. She thought many were taken to Northshore Medical Center in Slidell, but she could not be certain.

The city of Slidell, about thirty miles northeast of New Orleans on the other side of Lake Pontchartrain, suffered extensive flooding. It's true that Tenet was working to hire helicopters, but at 8:27 a.m. on Thursday, there were at least a hundred patients still at Memorial, including Bob. Most of the staff stayed all day Thursday and some didn't leave until Friday. Patients who did get out were being taken to a variety of hospitals, to the airport, or sometimes to other staging points to wait for transportation out. My sister Liz next tried to learn the name of the private company whose helicopters Tenet hired, hoping to get information from them about destinations. Her email at 9:40 a.m. Thursday described the response to that simple question:

> I hit a dead end. Got transferred to Tenet Gulf Coast regional office (contact Melanie) to try to find out what private firms were hired to do the evacuation. She had no idea who was responsible for booking the helicopters or how to find that info out. They are in crisis mode trying to get patients and staff out and have been working with Navy, Coast Guard, and LA Office of Emergency Preparedness. They were attempting to land helicopters this morning (concerned about her use of the word attempting...). She sounded completely harried and frantic and just said she could not help me.

Bob's nephew Randy in Dallas wrote an email on Thursday at 9:45 a.m. describing the communication problems Tenet and its hospitals were having:

> I was just on phone with Melanie. The only communication she has with Slidell is thru a satellite phone there that can make outgoing calls. She said the hospital in Slidell is operating like a M.A.S.H. unit and has been resupplied with water, meds, etc. (also National Guard) to care for patients. She would love to help but she is in the dark almost as much as we are.

Tenet Headquarters had finally concluded that government agencies were not going to rescue the people trapped at Memorial, and Tenet did manage to hire private helicopters. Before any of those could land, Coast Guard helicopters suddenly appeared at Memorial early Thursday morning and flew some patients and family members out. I believe now that I was a passenger on one of those Coast Guard flights. But no one apparently knew where any of the helicopters were going, and official systems that were in place to govern hospital transfers of patients were being ignored out of necessity. According to my searching relatives, Louis Armstrong International Airport was not mentioned by Tenet, on the phone or on its website, nor was it named as a drop point on other web sites that day, despite the fact that hundreds of patients, family members, and hospital employees from all over the city had been landing there steadily all that Thursday and in the days following.

In the baggage area of the airport, a slick film of wetness covered the hard tiles, as if the floor had been covered with water and a residue was left. The only light came from the large glass windows and open doors. I found a bench near the door where I'd come in, and I sat down to wait for the helicopter that would be bringing Bob. Soon a middle-aged man sat down next to me. He had gray-streaked hair and a ruddy complexion, and he told me he was accompanying his mother, one of the wheelchair patients. They'd been evacuated from a hospital in

Chalmette, a community between New Orleans and Slidell that had been inundated by the flood.

We waited.

At least an hour passed. I stared out toward the tarmac. Refugees from the storm were being disgorged by helicopters and brought to the door. Some walked under their own power, most of them dressed in surgical scrubs, sweat-stained and rumpled, with IDs hung around their necks. Some arrived in groups, looking weary in the stifling, heavy air. Mostly, though, the people coming through the doors needed help. Soon the line of wheelchairs snaked from the door toward the center of the room, the chairs filled with patients of various ages, silent and waiting.

Men and women in military fatigues pushed more wheelchairs to the back of the growing line, sometimes bending to speak a quiet word to the patients slumped in the chairs. The floor around the baggage carousels began to fill up with brown, military-type stretchers, each bearing a body, almost all in wrinkled hospital gowns, some partially covered by damp sheets, others with bare limbs sticking out from dirty gowns. Many patients looked old, and many looked sick.

A hum filled the cavernous room. Most patients on the stretchers were docile and quiet, but occasionally a voice cut through the din. By the far wall, a frail gray-haired woman called out for water. In the middle distance, an old bony black man writhed on his stretcher, calling out "Lord, have mercy on me, Lord, have mercy," over and over. Near the shiny steel baggage carousel, a lumpy, pink-cheeked woman cried out for her pill.

A few medics wearing orange vests identifying them as a Disaster Medical Team moved among the patients, asking them what they'd been hospitalized for, assessing status. They didn't give out medications, had no supplies—they simply made notes on clipboards. Other uniformed people rushed from the door toward the stairway in the distance. Near me, a woman on a stretcher cried that she wanted water, and a man in the middle of the group took up her chant, "Water, water." No one paid any attention, and no one seemed to have any water.

After awhile, a husky man in shorts stacked two flats of water bottles on the floor near our bench. I got up and gave the woman near me a bottle of water, and my bench mate, whom I had come to think of as "the man from Chalmette," handed a bottle to the male patient, but the old woman at the far wall was hard to reach. We'd have to weave through many stretchers to get to her. The entire floor was thick with bodies on stretchers, all lying in haphazard rows. I feared getting in the way and being ordered to leave. Instead of taking water to her, I tried to get a medic's attention, but I had no luck. Finally, the woman stopped asking for water and became quiet. This memory haunts me—I should have taken her some water.

The huge room was filling with people, and with noise, and the temperature was rising. The man from Chalmette and I talked to patients near us, trying to reassure them. Suddenly, the lumpy woman loudly demanded a pain pill. A medic went over and told her there were no pills, she'd have to wait. A few minutes later, she announced that she was going to have a bowel movement. Again the medic told her she had to wait. They didn't have bedpans, and the rest rooms were at the far end of the hall, across many yards of slippery floor. The woman got increasingly agitated. We tried to calm her. No one came to help her, and eventually she got quiet.

What kind of medical disaster team was this, I wondered, that didn't have basic supplies? If they're bringing patients here, why aren't they prepared to deal with basic needs like pain pills and bedpans? These are descendants of the people who planned D-Day and stormed the beaches at Normandy, who fought World War II and Korea. Where was the American ingenuity, the leadership, the ability to organize and improvise? How can these medics just walk around with clipboards and tell people they can't help them?

I thought of Bob, sitting alone in his wheelchair, getting smaller and smaller as my helicopter rose. Where was he? Had he gotten out yet? It had been more than an hour. Why wasn't he here?

Off to my left, stretcher bearers set down two stretchers holding a bedraggled white-haired couple, both at least in their seventies, maybe older. They wore rumpled shorts and sweaty tee-shirts, dirty canvas sneakers on their feet. Their skin was blotched red from sunburn. A young man followed, carrying their walker and canes.

"Here you go, Mister Sam. Got your walker here. You just relax, you and the missus are safe and we're gonna get you out. Don't you be giving no trouble now."

"Trouble? I ain't no trouble, you the trouble."

"What you mean? I carried you off that roof, didn't I? You're not gonna thank me?" The young man's tone was teasing.

"Yeah, I'll thank you, and I'll thank that Coast Guard. Now, I gotta use the bathroom." He sat up and moved to get off the stretcher.

"Okay, okay, Mister Sam. Hold on. I'll find somebody. You wait here now." The rescuer walked away, smiling.

The man from Chalmette seemed to recognize the couple, or maybe their accents, and spoke to them: "Are y'all from St. Bernard?"

"Arabi," she answered. "They took us off our roof." She sat up.

"Why did you stay in your house?" I asked.

"He wouldn't leave," she said, hooking her thumb toward her mate. "Old fool!" She spoke with warmth.

"Yeah, yeah," he muttered. "Where we gonna go, woman? Tell me that. Not leaving my house for no hurricane. Not Betsy, not Katrina."

"You leaving now, though."

I tried to picture the two of them, stuck for three days on the roof of their house, still in good spirits and jovial. I wondered whether Bob and I would be bantering affectionately with each other if that happened to us. I thought probably we would.

A young woman volunteer came over and helped Mister Sam to his feet, saying she'd help him to the rest room. She spoke with a similar accent and told them she'd grown up in St. Bernard Parish. She and Mr. Sam walked slowly and laboriously over the slick floor—it took them at least fifteen minutes to get there. When they returned, the same volunteer helped the wife to make the same laborious trip to the bathroom.

The day was more than half over, and still no sign of Bob. It was time to check upstairs, and if he wasn't there, somehow I'd get back down here to keep waiting. On my way to the stairs, I encountered a woman in military fatigues and asked her if all the wheelchair patients would be taken upstairs. "Yes," she replied, her tone confident, so I kept walking.

Reaching the top of the wide marble stairs, I entered one of the vast lobbies of the terminal. It had become a giant holding cell. Crowds of people, alone or in groups, sweltering in the hundred-plus degree temperatures, were arrayed all over the floor, sitting, lying, waiting. In an arcade of shops, patients slumped on wheelchairs or lay on stretchers, some with caregivers, many alone. Everyone looked hot and miserable. A gigantic mural hanging over the lobby entrance depicted legendary New Orleans musicians in gay colors of red, blue, and gold, blowing trumpets, trombones and clarinets, holding drumsticks, plucking a bass or singing into microphones. The mural loomed over the scene of loss and desperation. No music today, only the drone of rising uncertainty and chaos.

The entrance to the arcade of shops was cordoned off, guarded by a stiff woman in a military uniform. I explained my search, and she let me through to look for Bob. I walked to a table where two middle-aged women were taking down names on a long list—I assumed they were Red Cross workers. I waited in line then told them I was looking for my husband, who would be coming from Memorial/Baptist Hospital. They added my name and his to their list. I asked what would be done with the list. "We don't know," said one—the answer of the week.

I walked through the crowds to another central lobby, searching faces as I went. Two tents had been set up in the middle, with large Red Cross signs indicating they were acute care areas. I could see medics inside, bent over patients on gurneys. The hum of conversation, punctuated by moans, hung in the background. These medics were working feverishly to help patients, though I couldn't get close enough to see what kinds of procedures were being done. I didn't see anyone I recognized from Memorial. Everyone I saw seemed dazed. Once again I was reminded of *M.A.S.H.* This airport where Bob and I had flown into and out of so many times was now transformed into a war zone. I read later that in the week following the levee breaks, an estimated 30,000 refugees passed through Armstrong International Airport on their way out of the city, some stuck there for days. A huge number of these were patients from New Orleans hospitals. Later, I heard one New Orleans physician say that in those days when the airport was used as a transfer point for evacuated hospital patients, an average of eight people died every hour.

Bob wasn't anywhere in the crowd, so I turned and walked back through the lobby and down the stairs. At the bottom, I spotted the emergency worker who had told me I wouldn't be allowed back down. Just let him try to stop me, I thought. This place is so chaotic, with nobody in charge and nobody knowing anything, he can't have the nerve to enforce such a ridiculous rule. I decided if he confronted me, now I really would pitch a fit. He noticed me, but he kept walking and didn't stop me, maybe because of my determined look. More likely, the black eye got me a pass.

I returned to my bench near the far carousel, next to the man from Chalmette. Not much had changed. Helicopters were still disgorging refugees, and the floor was even more crowded with stretchers. Now stretchers holding patients in rumpled hospital gowns were being placed atop the baggage carousels that normally held luggage. Wheelchairs were lined up all along one wall. None of the chairs held Bob.

Another hour passed. Scanning faces, all at once I recognized a patient from our group at Memorial—he'd been with us that morning in the garage. He had oxygen tubes in his nose, but no oxygen tanks. I heard him tell a passing medic that he would need oxygen later, but the medic didn't seem hopeful that any would be available. The patient rose from his wheelchair, walked over, and sat on a bench near me. I moved closer to him.

"Hello," I said. "You were in Baptist hospital, weren't you? I remember you from the garage. Did you leave there in a helicopter?"

"Yeah," he said, and seemed to recognize me too.

"I was with my husband, and I had to leave before him. Did you by any chance see if he got on a helicopter? He was bald, glasses, in a wheelchair."

"Yeah, I remember him, I saw you both together," he said, nodding, "but he wasn't on my 'copter, and I didn't see him go. Sorry. Only thing I can tell you is I heard them say the next 'copter after ours was going to Lakefront Airport."

"Lakefront?" All this time, I had assumed they'd be bringing all the patients here. What if they took Bob to another airport? I don't know if any helicopters actually landed at Lakefront Airport that day—so much of that area on the shore of Lake Pontchartrain was flooded—but now this news startled me. I'd been waiting for more than four hours. Time had crawled, and it seemed far longer. I felt as if I'd been stuck in that airport for days. Now Bob might not be coming here at all. A rising panic gripped me.

How much longer should I wait? Restless, I picked up my purse and tote and started walking toward the marble steps. I'd check upstairs again.

Just outside the cordoned area, in a crowd of stretchers clustered in front of The Body Shop, I spotted a man with hair the color of Bob's. My breath caught, but when I got closer, it wasn't him. And I'd forgotten—Bob didn't have white hair now, he had no hair. What was I thinking? In a way, I was glad it wasn't Bob—this patient looked so alone. I hoped Bob had somebody with him, wherever he was.

I wandered the lobby. By now I had asked three different people with uniforms if they knew where wheelchair patients were being taken. Each one had given me a different answer. The first had said adamantly that they all would eventually be taken upstairs. The second said that wasn't true, they'd stay on the lower level. A third said nobody knew where anybody was going.

What should I do? Should I try to get out? If I left, they might still bring Bob here. So many of these patients were alone, with no caregivers, and the medics were clearly overwhelmed. I couldn't stand the thought of Bob here by himself in this chaos, with me gone and no one to help him. But if I stayed, I could be stuck here and Bob might be somewhere else, somewhere worse. Would they have taken him to the Superdome? A crowded shelter? Maybe I should try to get out, get to a phone, rent a car, somehow come back to find him, do something. Here, I was helpless.

I returned to the gatekeeper of the cordoned-off area, standing like Cerberus guarding the entrance to Hades, and told her my story. She urged me to get myself out, if I could. She told me to go back to the terminal area and stand in line for a flight. Still agonizing over whether to leave, I walked back to the lobby, finally deciding if I were stuck here and Bob didn't come, I'd be helpless to find him. A long line had formed at the entrance to one of the security gates leading to Concourse C. I got at the end and asked people ahead of me if they knew where the line was going.

"Atlanta," said one.

"Houston," said another.

"Nobody knows," said a third, again the answer of the day.

We waited. Suddenly word spread through the line that it was necessary to get on a FEMA list before we'd be able to board a flight. I'd heard that acronym a lot over the past week. I knew it was a federal disaster response agency, and I'd seen its officials giving reassuring interviews on TV as the hurricane approached. Where had they been in the past four days? Later, we would all learn more than we wanted to know about FEMA and its failures. Now a number of people left the line, turning to walk back toward the staircase and into an adjoining lobby. Unsure whether to follow them, I walked a short distance to a central desk where a man sat under a large sign that said *Information*.

As I approached, I suppose looking hopeful, he told me, "I have very little information."

"Do you know whether there's a FEMA list I have to get on to get out?"

He shook his head. "There's no list. Just stand in that line and you *might* get on a plane. No guarantee, but if you want to leave, that's the best way."

So I re-joined the line. Most of the people around me were staff from area hospitals, many wearing scrubs. Two large women wearing badges from a Chalmette hospital were pulling huge black rolling suitcases behind them, which they'd apparently been allowed to bring onto helicopters. Fury shot through me—how come they could bring those huge bags when my two small sacks were snatched from my hands?

Now another rumor spread through the line. A bus was leaving for Baton Rouge from a door by the ticket desks. Several people left our line and headed for the other lobby. The man and woman directly in front of me discussed whether to try for that bus—he was hoping to get to friends in Baton Rouge—but they decided to stay in line. I told them I would, too—being stuck on a bus could waste precious time. If I could fly somewhere else, I could start searching for Bob. They had been evacuated from Lindy Boggs Medical Center, another Tenet facility in New Orleans, and when they heard my story, they gave me an 800 number for Tenet headquarters and suggested I call when I got to a phone. They thought it was likely patients from Memorial would be taken to other Tenet hospitals. The tall, bright-eyed woman was an administrator and the young man wearing owlish spectacles worked in the pharmacy at Lindy Boggs. That hospital in Mid-City had also been flooded, and their ordeal over the past several days sounded similar to our experience at Memorial—they too had been trapped for days in the terrible heat, stranded with their patients, surrounded by water.

Everyone in the line waited patiently—by now we were all used to waiting—uncertain whether we'd get on a plane and if we did, where it would go. At the other side of the lobby, in front of the airport's Acme Oyster House, workers began handing out free Meals Ready to Eat. The word spread, and we held each others' places in line to walk across to get food. The pharmacist explained that the

MREs had a little heating system built in and once you opened them, you had hot food. Alas, there were no oyster poor boys at this Acme. I was given a shoebox-sized, brown plastic package labeled "Vegetarian Pasta." Although I was hungry, I was too nervous to eat it. The fatigue, the uncertainty, the terrible heat: I couldn't face food. So I put the MRE in my tote. I'd save it—maybe Bob and I could share it as we reminisced about Katrina.

Sometime later, my neighbors kept my place while I left the line to visit a nearby Ladies' Room. Toilets were still working at the airport, thank goodness—I estimated that at least a thousand people were gathered on this level alone. Outside the bathroom, three teenage girls were huddled on the floor around an electrical cord leading to an outlet that must have been working, all trying to charge their cell phones.

"Do your cell phones work?" I asked them.

"Not yet," said one of the girls. "People say some phones might work, though, if they charge."

It didn't sound hopeful. I decided not to bother and returned to the line.

More time passed. We waited. Without any air conditioning or ventilation, the lobby sweltered. My tee shirt stuck to my back. My skin felt sweaty and gritty. By now it was late afternoon. After my restless lack of sleep in the garage and the hours of tension today, standing in line got harder. Looking up, I saw the huge gilded figure of Icarus hanging from the airport ceiling, greeting travelers arriving in and leaving New Orleans. It made me think of the Auden poem about suffering, and about Icarus drowning while all around him people went about their business, unconcerned. I resolved to look that poem up and read it again if I ever got out. Where were the rescuers? Why were we all still stuck here, four days after the storm? Why were there no plans in place to care for the people stranded in this airport and in the city? And what was happening to Bob?

At that point a man facing us at the head of the line loudly announced that anyone carrying a weapon of any kind should bring it forward and arrange to mail it out, no questions asked. A young man in line not far ahead of me pulled a pistol out of his knapsack, and a number of others stepped up to the gate and handed over knives and guns. I wonder now what happened to those weapons, since mail shut down in New Orleans for months after the levees breached. Is there a pile of abandoned guns and knives still stashed somewhere in a forgotten corner of Louis Armstrong International Airport?

A few minutes later, the line started to move. We were told the plane would be going to Atlanta, news the crowd greeted with little comment. The destination didn't seem important—everybody just wanted to get out. Agents at the Security table were a laid-back group, checking bags perfunctorily and sending us one by one through a metal detector. I didn't notice whether the detector was actually working. With power off, it's possible our going through the detector was a sham. We gave our names for a list and were asked our final destination. I said I didn't know until I learned where my husband had been taken, so they put a question mark by my name. No one was asked to show any ID.

Once through security, I walked down the long concourse that seemed surreally familiar. This hallway had windows, and outside it was grey and pouring rain again. My stitches throbbed, and I knew my varicolored eye was the first thing people noticed when they looked at me. When I reached the gate, a young man with a FEMA badge hurried over and asked if he could help me. To my surprise, I burst into tears, making him even more solicitous as I told him I needed to find my husband who had been a patient at Memorial Hospital. He carried my tote and helped me outside and across the tarmac in the rain to the rolling staircase leading to a Delta plane.

"There will be people in Atlanta to help you," he said. "Just tell them what you need."

I climbed the stairs, wet from the pouring rain, still not sure if leaving was the right thing to do, still worried Bob might be brought here and be alone. But the crowd was growing, the airport was a grim scene and getting grimmer, and there was no knowing how many flights would leave. I told myself while I had this chance, I had to get out.

Inside the door of the plane, the Delta crew stood at their normal places, welcoming each of us with smiles though their eyes were pinched with concern. My fellow passengers and I filed in, a rag-tag, grungy, stinky bunch, most of us having gone at least three days without soap and water, much less a bath. I had a moment of amusement, thinking that these were the dirtiest clothes I'd ever worn on a plane, and I'd never flown without underwear.

An attendant announced that anyone who was a nurse was invited to sit at the front of the plane—a nice touch, I thought—and the rest of us chose seats in the back section. I sat in a row with the young pharmacist and bright-eyed administrator from Lindy Boggs, and we each found in our seats a blanket and a kit containing toothbrush, toothpaste, comb, and other sundries, like the kits airlines give business travelers. What luxury it would be to use a toothbrush. The plane's air conditioner was going full blast, and the cool air felt heavenly. I sank into the seat, the first padded chair in days—I'd complained about airline seats in the past, but this one felt like utter comfort. Waiting, I had fantasized that the seat-back might contain a phone I could use, but no luck. It was some consolation knowing that all the family would be searching, but I couldn't wait to get to Atlanta and to a phone.

I hadn't been on many planes without Bob. We had always had to fly on tiny commuter planes in and out of central Pennsylvania to larger hubs, and I'd grip Bob's hand on takeoffs and landings and during frequent mid-air bumps and dips. We'd had some harrowing winter flights in ice and snow and wind. Over the years we'd both grown less and less fond of flying, even on larger jets, but we still loved to travel, so we steeled ourselves and boarded the planes. We'd made a list of trips we wanted to take when chemo was over and Bob was better: a return to the English Lake District, which we both loved, and a visit to Italy, to see the mosaics in the basilica at Ravenna and re-visit Venice. And somehow we'd find a way to fulfill a longing Bob had had for decades: to see the battlefield at Troy. But the first stop for me would be Atlanta, and on this flight today I was more than ready to leave. I only wished Bob were next to me.

Looking out the window as the plane took off, I gazed down at waterlogged New Orleans. The Mississippi followed its normal crescent-shaped path—the earthen levees along the river had held. Lake Pontchartrain looked anything but normal. The lake's coastline had expanded, swallowing up streets and neighborhoods, and houses seemed to float like boats on the water. I felt an inexpressible relief to be in the air and getting away, but also an overwhelming pain looking down at the city. How long would it be before we saw New Orleans again? Would the city survive this deluge? And where was Bob? Was he still down there somewhere, trapped by the water?

The flight attendants were kind, walking the aisle, talking to people, reassuring any who were troubled—in a seat across the aisle from me, an elderly black woman with frightened eyes behind big glasses looked near tears. For some of the evacuees, this may have been their first airplane flight. We learned later that every Delta evacuation flight in those days after the flood had a volunteer crew. The highlight of the flight for me and for my seatmates was when they served us soft drinks containing *ice*. Never had ice cubes tasted so wonderful. I savored every one.

The flight was short. Landing in Atlanta, we were surprised to see the plane taxi not to the terminal but to a remote, grassy corner of the airfield. My seatmates and I speculated about the reason.

"We're all too dirty to be allowed in the terminal," said the spectacled pharmacist.

"And we probably smell too ripe," I said. "We'd stink up the place."

"The first thing I'm heading for is a shower," said the Lindy Boggs administrator.

We were all helped off the plane and greeted by several people waiting at the bottom of a roll-away staircase. "Welcome to Atlanta," they said—we might have been visiting dignitaries. I had a sudden fantasy of being handed a bouquet of roses, but instead the greeters all looked at us with pity. We were guided to waiting buses, which after a ride of a few minutes delivered us to a nearby Holiday Inn. About a dozen people milled around at the front of the hotel, all wearing FEMA badges. At least FEMA's doing something here, I thought. The greeters offered each of us a sack containing a Chick-Fil-A sandwich and fries—hot!—and told us we'd be given rooms for the night and then helped to get wherever we wanted to go next.

My first priority was a phone. I was directed to a short Asian woman who seemed to be in charge. "Is there a phone I can use?' I asked. "My husband was a hospital patient. He was taken out separately from me. I don't know where he is, and I have to find him."

"Come with me," she said, and ushered me into an office, where she moved a chair next to a table holding a phone. "Here are some Delta phone cards you can use for long distance," she said. "If you need more, let me know."

I snatched up the receiver and heard the comforting buzz of a dial tone. I punched in the card access numbers then my brother's number in Raleigh. He answered on the first ring.

"Bill, it's Carolyn." Before I could say more, he cut in, knowing instinctively what I'd want to hear first.

"Thank God. We know where Bob is. We talked to him, and he's okay, in a hospital in Thibodaux, Louisiana. Where are you?"

For the second time that day, I broke down in tears, this time tears of relief.

It turned out that Bob had been flown out of Magnolia Garage not long after I left. His helicopter took him directly to Thibodaux Regional Medical Center, about sixty-five miles southwest of New Orleans, where he arrived with other patients from flooded area hospitals. Miraculously, Bob's chart stayed with him. Doctors told us later that many patients arrived with no charts, no information about diagnosis or treatment, no contact numbers.

Hospital officials immediately called the first of the family numbers I'd listed in his chart, and Bob was able to talk to our sister-in-law Samantha, Bill's wife. She reported that he sounded "weak but okay." Bob was worried about

117

me—he told her he saw me leave and didn't know where I'd been taken. That afternoon, Bob managed to call again, asking my brother Bill if he'd heard from me. Worried that I might still be stuck at Memorial, Bill questioned Bob again, and Bob reported that he had seen me actually on the helicopter, a small one. Bill explained that there were many shelters, and they'd probably have to wait for me to call, but the moment anyone heard from me, someone would let Bob know. Bill emailed the family that Bob "sounded pretty good—better than I had feared."

I could imagine the worry and tension Bob had been feeling ever since we were told we'd be separated, and especially after he watched me leave him in the garage. Bob had an innate fear of being lost. I had discovered soon after we met that he had absolutely no sense of direction and an almost total inability to orient himself in geographic space. Even standing in a place he knew well, he couldn't point to North or South. He could walk into a store and within minutes have no idea which way he came in, or how to get out. It had nothing to do with intelligence or concentration—he just lacked some basic navigational instinct. Once when he was sitting in his office, a new student advisee asked where the library was. Bob pointed in a direction exactly opposite to the true location on campus and then confessed he had no idea. When he drove a car, he had to rely on maps and signs or memorize landmarks—he'd been one of the first in line when satellite navigational systems were new. He told me he inherited the "directionless gene" from his mother—she'd had the same inability to feel her way in space. We laughed about it and decided it was one more reason we were right for each other: I could navigate intuitively and usually managed to get us to our destination. But this limitation troubled him. When my sense of direction occasionally failed and we did get lost, Bob would always be extremely nervous. He hated not knowing where he was. Being carried up those stairs to the helipad and flying into the unknown—alone—must have disturbed him terribly.

Bill gave me Bob's phone number in his hospital room in Thibodaux so I could call him directly. Hearing him answer the phone nearly started the waterworks again. But I managed to sound upbeat and tell him I would spend the night in Atlanta and get to him, somehow, the next day. I could tell by his voice that he was relieved to hear me, too.

"How are you?" I asked.

"I'm okay," he said. "Just come soon—and be careful."

I called the main office at the Medical Center there, and they told me the nearest airport was in Lafayette. The man I spoke to gave me driving directions and assured me I would be able to stay in Bob's room with him.

Next I went to the hotel's reception desk and was assigned a room on the third floor. It was an old-style Holiday Inn, with rooms opening onto an outside balcony, and all around me shell-shocked evacuees were opening doors to rooms or wandering the corridors, looking dazed. Some clutched cold drinks from vending machines or carried buckets of ice. In my room, I cranked up the air conditioner to full-blast and stood for several minutes directly in front of the fan, letting the cold air wash over me. Then I spent an hour calling various family, telling them I was in Atlanta and okay. "Thank God you're safe. Atlanta? How in the world did you end up there?" was the general reaction.

The moment she'd heard the news from our brother, my sister Lorraine (among the family we called her Rainy), a master organizer, had begun arranging a flight out for me, and she phoned to tell me I had a ticket the next day for an early afternoon flight from Atlanta to Lafayette, where she had managed to book a rental car for pickup at the Lafayette airport. She estimated the ninety-five mile drive would get me to Thibodaux by late afternoon. I would be with Bob in less than twenty-four hours.

Finally, I was able to relax a bit, and even to enjoy being comfortable for the first time in more than four days. I devoured the chicken sandwich, reveled in the air conditioning, and got a huge bucket of ice from the dispenser in a nearby stairwell. I shed my filthy clothes and tried to wash them with the small bar of hotel soap. Then I filled the tub and soaked in a hot bath, after which I also stood under the shower. It felt indescribably good to be clean.

Sinking into the luxury of the real bed, with its crisp, clean sheets, I realized I was exhausted. Before trying to sleep, however, I turned on the TV. For the first time, I got a sense of all that had been happening—and not happening—in New Orleans over the past four days. We had been isolated in the hospital, our world limited to the garage and surrounding streets. I was thankful to hear reports that the French Quarter had escaped flooding. I hadn't let myself think much about the house we'd worked so long to renovate and loved so much. Now I realized it would be okay. We could go back.

Yet the TV reports were grim. I was aghast to hear of the horrors happening all over the city, the chaos in the Superdome, the accounts of people drowning or being rescued from their flooded homes in boats, the crowds still stuck on highway overpasses, the looting and violence the media were already focusing on. For the first time, I got a sense of the widespread destruction and suffering caused by the failed levees and the shocking lack of response by government agencies. I heard replays of Mayor Nagin's outraged radio interview, demanding help for the battered city. I saw the thousands of refugees huddled in front of the Convention Center, with no water, no food, no medicine, and no shelter from the brutal heat. I learned that the aftermath of the collapsed federally-built flood walls and levees was far, far worse than the storm itself. I fell asleep that night feeling lucky to have escaped, those haunting lyrics still echoing in my head:

Just a little change, small to say the least
Both a little scared, neither one prepared....

Chapter Seven

The Only Place On My Map

Friday, September 2

In the morning, FEMA hosted a breakfast for all evacuees in one of the Atlanta hotel's large meeting rooms. The night before, there'd been a televised admonition from one of the politically correct pundits, lecturing the nation not to call us "refugees," but I certainly felt like a refugee.

I'd awakened early, ready for the day and the trip to Bob. The shirt, bra, and slacks I'd worn for four days and washed last night weren't entirely dry, but they were all I had, so I put them on anyway. Passing by the mirror in the morning light, I was startled by the stranger I saw there. Who was that bedraggled woman with grungy, rumpled clothes—and still no underpants—who looked as if she'd been through several rounds of a boxing match? Under the smudged bandage, a row of black stitches stuck up from the wound above my eye. The eye was streaked with shades of purple and yellow, and a purplish bruise covered my upper cheek and part of my forehead. I looked a mess.

No matter how I looked, I had to get moving, and I made my way to the breakfast room. The FEMA people in Atlanta seemed organized and ready to respond, unlike what was happening in New Orleans. People who needed temporary housing in Atlanta were given information and guidance, and those of us who wanted to keep traveling were helped with planning. In addition to the FEMA workers, we found a roomful of smiling representatives and volunteers from various charitable organizations trying to assist the ragged group of evacuees: people of all ages, alone like me or in family groups, all looking stunned and distant-eyed after the ordeal they'd been through.

121

At the corners of the breakfast room, tables were heaped with donated clothing. A motherly, cluck-clucking volunteer came over to me as I was eating an egg sandwich and fingered the sleeve of my stained tee shirt, still damp and looking moldy. I was sure she had zeroed in on my colorful eye.

"We need to get you a shirt," she said.

"Really, I'm okay," I said. "This one will dry soon. But thanks."

"Leave your food and come with me," she said. "You can come back and finish." She stood there until I got up.

She led me over to one of the tables and ordered me to take a shirt. I'd never before accepted this kind of charity, and it felt odd. But in the last few days I'd gotten used to doing as I was told, and it would be comforting to wear something besides the damp, dirty shirt I'd had on for four days. There seemed to be plenty of clothes, so I picked out a bright yellow polo shirt and felt like a grateful refugee. After breakfast, I stopped in the hotel's gift shop and bought some underwear, a small pack of strip bandages, and a souvenir "Atlanta Peach" tee shirt to have as a spare. The night before, most evacuees leaving the buses had been given new tee shirts bearing the logo of the Atlanta Falcons, the longtime NFL rival of the New Orleans Saints. I'd been intent on finding a phone and missed that giveaway. Many at breakfast were wearing those clean shirts, rivals or not.

A FEMA representative had come by my breakfast table and asked about my plans. I explained that my sister had reserved a ticket on a flight to Lafayette so I could rejoin my husband. She checked with Delta to make sure that reservation was confirmed—it was—and told me FEMA would cover the cost of the ticket as well as last night's room. So despite all the well-earned complaints I heard about FEMA in the days after the levee breaches, and the justified criticism that escalated as the city and its citizens struggled to rebound, I have to admit that I did get at least this personal benefit from my Homeland Security tax dollars. FEMA put me up for a night and flew me from Atlanta to Lafayette. As a travel agency, FEMA worked. As a disaster relief organization, its performance was itself a complete disaster.

I had some time before my flight, so I went back to my room, where there was a message from my brother. His law firm had an office in Atlanta, and he had arranged for a colleague to take me to a nearby mall and then to the airport. As I waited in front of the hotel, a middle-aged blond woman came over and asked me in a slow Georgia drawl if I had come from New Orleans. When I said yes, her eyebrows knitted in a frown.

"Do you need cash?" she said, pulling a wallet out of her purse. "Let me give you some money to tide you over. I feel so sorry for all of you. I wish there were more we could do." With my wrinkled clothes and ragged appearance, I must have looked as homeless as I felt.

"Thank you so much," I said, "but really, I'm fine. I got out with some cash. But I'm sure there are people inside who could use it." My eye was getting me all kinds of attention. How odd to be pressed to take money from a complete stranger. "You're kind to offer."

She looked dubious. "Are you sure?"

I assured her I had plenty and thanked her again, and she moved toward the hotel lobby. The concern and caring of everyone I encountered in Atlanta was comforting. People all over the country had been watching the terrible suffering unfold on their TV screens, feeling helpless and angry, I was sure, at the government's bungling and lack of response. The past four days had given me some lessons in feeling helpless and angry.

At the mall, I bought a new pair of slacks and some socks, and my brother's colleague insisted I choose a small duffel bag as a gift from the firm. I felt presentable when I walked through the bustling, normal-seeming Atlanta terminal and boarded the Delta flight to Lafayette. I learned that my flight on Thursday was one of the few that had left the chaotic New Orleans airport all that day, so I was lucky to have gotten on it. Again I was struck by how luxurious this plane's air conditioning felt. The cool air was bliss.

Landing at Lafayette in mid-afternoon, I went to the Hertz desk to pick up my rental car but was told that although they did have a reservation for me, they didn't have a car. Vehicles were in short supply all over the state of Louisiana, and as rentals were returned to the airport, the Hertz people would assign them to new renters according to a waiting list. So, I added my name to the list and settled in for more waiting.

At least my cell phone worked sporadically, and I was able to talk to my sister Rainy, who had let Bob know I was driving from Lafayette. Rainy said phones in Thibodaux were often down. Bob could get calls from outside but couldn't phone out. Later, that would be reversed, with lines overloaded in the entire area. Family would have to wait for us to call out, getting only recorded "all circuits busy" messages when they tried to phone us. Today, my cell phone worked only fitfully, and I wasn't able to reach Bob directly. But Rainy told me Bob had sounded much better than she expected—he said it was "a nice little hospital" and he was getting good care. She would try to get word to him that I was delayed but on the way. I worried about his condition: how hard had the helicopter evacuation been for him? How much longer before I got to him?

The workers at the Hertz desk were trying hard to accommodate everyone who wanted a car and were strictly following their waiting list. Cars trickled in, but after more than an hour, the truck supposedly bringing a supply of vehicles still hadn't arrived. I checked with them periodically, trying to be patient but making sure they remembered I was waiting, and telling them I was trying to get to my hospitalized husband. At one point, I looked straight at the dark-haired young woman and the fair-haired young man dressed in black and yellow uniforms behind the counter and half-jokingly tried to play on their sympathy.

"Hey, don't you think this eye should get me some special treatment?" I asked.

They smiled, and the young man said, "That's pretty impressive. Does it hurt?"

"Not much. Just thought I'd try," I said, grinning.

"We're going to get you a car just as soon as we can," he said.

"Look, you've moved up the list," said the girl, showing me my name, now third on the list.

I waited some more, watching as two more people came into the airport, handed in keys, and their vehicles were reassigned to new drivers. I wondered how many rental cars Bob and I had driven over the years. Dozens and dozens, maybe close to a hundred, I mused, from various companies. Overseas, though, we had usually rented from Hertz, probably because it was such a well-established company with outlets everywhere. And overseas we always made sure we had plenty of insurance. I could still see the British Hertz agent, wearing the familiar black and yellow, giving me a look of astounded horror the first time we rented a car in London and I asked a question that seemed quite logical to me. Knowing that in Britain cars drove on the left side of roads and were built with steering wheels on the right, I looked at the two pedals on the floor next to the gas pedal and wondered if the clutch and brake were also placed differently from those in American cars.

"Which one is the brake?" I asked, pointing to the pedals and eliciting that horrified look.

For a moment I thought he was going to tear up our rental contract and refuse to trust us with a car. In the end he accepted my explanation, and Bob's insistence that we both did know how to drive a stick shift. Still, the agent watched warily as we drove off.

"I'm fighting the temptation to pop the clutch and jerk out into the Edgware Road," said Bob, with mischief in his eye.

"He ought to be glad at least I asked," I said, and we both giggled.

I was wondering what kind of rental car I'd get this time, and wishing Bob were going to be in the passenger seat, when the Hertz workers called out my name at last. There was genuine gladness in both agents' faces as they handed me the keys to a four-door Chevy sedan, pointed to the lot outside, and wished me luck.

Finally, I turned out of the airport exit onto Highway 90, headed for the Thibodaux Regional Medical Center. I'd driven this highway before between Lafayette and New

Orleans. Bob and I sometimes had taken this road as an alternate on our drives to and from Houston. Except for the October night of oysters and music and celebration we'd had in Lafayette, those drives had been tense trips, both of us dreading the ordeal Bob would face at the destination. I'd seen the exit signs for Thibodaux, but until now I'd never envisioned going there.

Now it was the only place on my map.

As I drove, everywhere I saw signs of the storm. Katrina's western edge had skirted this part of the state, moving more towards the east. Still, the storm had left its mark along the road: giant billboards and signs with slats blown out, dangling loosely; trees bent and broken; pools of water standing in fields; brown mud splashed on walls of the gas stations and fast-food restaurants lining the highway.

Dusk was deepening as I took the turnoff to Thibodaux, and in what seemed like minutes, it was dark. Now the road was unfamiliar, and I switched on the map light and glanced at my written directions, dictated over the phone by a hospital administrator. I tried to memorize the route, my back aching and eyes squinting to see the highway signs. After a wrong turn, backtracking, and stopping at a 7-Eleven for confirmation of the directions I was following, I finally came to the outskirts of Thibodaux. I crossed the bridge over Bayou Lafourche near the town center, passed the sign to Nichols State University, and spotted the boxy grey building that must be the hospital. I parked in the lot and half-ran to an open door where light poured out: the ER. Directed to another door, I left and retraced my steps. Through the main hospital entrance I entered a dark, silent lobby and moved past an information desk with its sign saying visiting hours were over.

The elevator to the third floor seemed to take forever but finally opened onto a long hallway guarded by a nurses' station. Behind the desk, two women in blue scrubs looked at me quizzically—their stares focused on my purple and yellow-streaked eye.

"Can we help you?" one of the nurses asked.

"I'm Carolyn Perry. My husband Robert Perry was brought here from Baptist Hospital in New Orleans."

"You made it!" said the pretty nurse with long, dark hair. "He's been waiting for you—Room 316." She pointed down the hallway.

Rushing down that hall, I pushed open the door to 316 and there he was: propped up in the hospital bed wearing a clean, blue-dotted gown. When Bob saw me, his face lit up with a huge smile.

"Hi," Bob said, giving it two syllables from the Texas twang that only rarely slipped into his speech. I will never forget the look on his face as I walked over and leaned down to give him a long hug. I stayed there awhile, my head on his shoulder and his arms around me, neither of us talking. Thank God I'd found him. I knew our ordeal wasn't over, but at least we could face whatever was next together.

Bob wanted to know all about what had happened to me, and I questioned him about his evacuation from Memorial. When his helicopter landed, he thought he was in Baton Rouge and expected to find me waiting there for him. "You weren't there, and I kept asking everybody where you were," he said.

"Well, don't sound so annoyed," I said. "It's not like I deserted you." I told him about my long hours in the airport, waiting, and my night in Atlanta. In our thirty-six years together, we hadn't spent many nights apart.

"It sounds as if our house is okay," I said. "The French Quarter didn't flood, thank heaven."

"You'll never guess who called me—Kelleigh," Bob said. A friend's daughter, whom we hadn't seen in years, had noticed our names listed among the missing on a CNN web site and somehow tracked Bob down in Thibodaux, talking to him before most of the family could get through. He was astonished to get her phone call. I have no idea how our names got on that web site—maybe my sisters had listed us, or maybe the list from the Red Cross table at the airport actually made it to the internet. Later, Bob's nephew Bill and brother George managed to get calls through, and we were able to reassure the family that we were both safe and reunited. Over the next days, we got unexpected phone calls from friends as the word of our whereabouts spread. Most touching, I got emails from several former students—in Pennsylvania, North Carolina, other states—hoping we were safe and offering us haven in their homes.

Whatever was in store for us next, at least neither of us would be alone. Those song lyrics from *Beauty and the Beast* still echoed: *Ever as before, ever just as sure, as the sun will rise.* Sleeping that night in a chair by Bob's bed, my hand touching his arm, I got my first truly restful sleep in a week.

Chapter Eight

These Are the Dog Days, Fortunatus

September 3 – 24

Everyone at Thibodaux Hospital seemed intent on welcoming evacuees and making us feel as comfortable as possible. Several doctors tended to Bob over the next week, and they discovered one of Bob's lungs had partially collapsed during the escape from Memorial, perhaps from the changes in air pressure in the helicopter, or just the physical stress of the evacuation. A procedure was done to correct it. He was also given intravenous antibiotics because he'd contracted an infection, hardly surprising after spending the night on the filthy floor of that garage.

Once Bob had partially recovered from the lung procedure, a Thibodaux oncologist took over his care. Dr. Ellis, a dark-haired man with glasses, a receding hairline, and a soothing voice, knew Dr. Veith and tried to contact him, but he was unable to reach Dr. Veith in the days after the flood. We learned that Dr. Veith's home near the lake in New Orleans had taken on water up to the roof. It was rumored that he made his way on foot and by boat through the floodwater to join physicians working at East Jefferson Hospital, one of the few hospitals still open in the area. Although we heard he was safe, we weren't able to contact him during our time in Thibodaux. But I had brought enough of Bob's recent records to help Dr. Ellis decide on treatment, and over the next week, Bob's condition stabilized.

I piled our few possessions in a corner of Bob's room, and at night I slept on the chair that folded out to make a bed of sorts. One of the Thibodaux doctors removed the stitches above my eye when it was time, but my colorful bruises continued to get pitying looks and a few curious "what happened to your eye?" questions from the nurses and other staff.

The small hospital, roughly sixty-five miles west and a bit south of New Orleans, was packed with patients from flooded hospitals, and a shelter for other evacuees had been set up in the nearby gymnasium of Nichols State University. When I ventured out of the hospital, driving the rental Chevy to a local shopping center or walking to a nearby supermarket, I encountered clumps of dazed-looking New Orleanians in the stores, speaking in recognizable accents and pushing carts full of clothing or food or Pampers, or supplies for cleaning or camping, all looking utterly disoriented. They made me think of an old *Saturday Night Live* skit with a punch line Bob and I often quoted to each other in all kinds of situations. Two characters played thieves living in an apartment full of loot. One night, they returned to their apartment, only to find that other burglars had broken in and stolen all their plunder. Their wide-eyed, disbelieving reaction to the empty apartment was, "Where *is* everything?" The faces of displaced New Orleanians showed the same disbelief.

After one excursion to purchase toiletries for me and a battery-powered razor and lightweight robe for Bob, I returned to the room and tried to give Bob a sense of the world outside the hospital.

"Bayou Lafourche runs right through the middle of Thibodaux," I said. "Even muddy, the water looked inviting today—it's unbelievably hot and humid out there. The sun is fierce."

"*Yes, these are the dog days, Fortunatus,*" said Bob, a favorite line from W. H. Auden's "Under Sirius" that Bob quoted often during sweltering Louisiana summers. "Just be glad you're out of that wretched garage."

"The town's full of Katrina refugees—I hope the shelters have air conditioning. We've got it pretty nice here in this hospital. Sure could've done worse."

Our plan was to return to M. D. Anderson in Houston as soon as Bob could travel, and I started making arrangements. Nurses told me they could arrange an ambulance to transfer Bob, and when I learned a furnished apartment was available in a complex near the clinic, I told Bob excitedly that things were looking up for us at last.

I was unprepared for the news we got on September 8, exactly a week after we'd escaped from Memorial. First, a nurse on the morning shift said plans for the ambulance were being canceled because a bed wasn't available for Bob at M. D. Anderson's hospital. Next, we learned a CAT scan had been scheduled. Earlier, we'd been told by Dr. Ellis that they wouldn't do a CAT scan in Thibodaux since it would just have to be duplicated in Houston. What was going on?

After lunch, Dr. Ellis entered the room with a somber expression on his face. He told us that M. D. Anderson was overwhelmed with evacuees and the hospital was full to overflowing. Besides, he had spoken at length with Bob's specialist in Houston. They had decided the present chemotherapy wasn't working, but Bob was too ill and weak to start any other. For the first time, in his slow, solemn voice, Dr. Ellis mentioned hospice. He said once Bob was stronger, he would have two options: try a new chemotherapy or do nothing, and enter a hospice program.

Bob looked stunned, and so was I. Hearing the word *hospice*, I reacted instantly: hospice was not an option. Hospice meant no hope. We were not at that point yet. The doctor had said there was another chemo we could try.

We didn't have to decide at once. "We can move you to rehab, and you can try to build up your strength," said the doctor.

All afternoon, Bob lay with a distant expression on his face and I sat numbly by his bed, both of us hardly speaking. At one point, Bob said, "I wonder how long I have?"

Awhile later, he said, "What a waste."

I'm not sure what he meant. At the time, I thought he was referring to the disease. The cancer had wrecked his body and ruined his future. He'd had such plans for his retirement years, so much more to do and to give. Before his diagnosis, he had loved his days volunteering at the aquarium, relishing his encounters with the animals and the people there, especially the children and school groups coming through. He had hoped to start a reading group to tutor and motivate young people at a community center near our house. And we looked forward to more travel and new adventures. To have his life cut short by this disease truly was a waste. Looking back, I think he may have been thinking of the sixteen months of chemo he'd endured, the precious time spent in hospitals and doctors' offices suffering through treatments that didn't work. Perhaps he meant both.

"I don't want you to give up, Bob," I said. "Doctors don't know everything. We've heard all those stories of people living longer than their doctors predict. Dr. Ellis said there's another chemo—don't you want to try it?"

"I'm not sure," he said. He seemed depressed. I felt like breaking down myself, but I'd save that for later, when I was alone. Now I focused on him.

"Well, there's time to decide," I said. "Let's just concentrate on getting you stronger. Rehab at least can make you feel better. And we can investigate the new chemo."

"Okay," he said. "I do want to try."

So that became our plan.

The next day, Bob moved to the Rehab Unit on the fourth floor of Thibodaux Regional Medical Center. It would become our home for the next three weeks.

At first, Bob shared a double room. I slept in a chair by his bed. The patient in the other bed, a thin African-American man from New Orleans who told us he was on kidney dialysis, was very ill and didn't talk much, but during one of his brief conversations, we learned he had been separated from his wife and family and didn't know where they were or how to find them. The nurses had assured him the hospital's social workers were looking, and we were relieved a few days later when he told us they'd found his wife and son in a shelter in Baton Rouge and he had been able to talk to them on the phone.

After two days, Bob was moved to a private room with a chair that converted to a makeshift bed, so I was able to sleep flat with a bit more privacy, a good thing since all motels in Thibodaux were filled with evacuees. Other spouses were also living in the Rehab Unit, and we learned that nearly all were from New Orleans and surrounding parishes. Some had evacuated before Katrina but others were forced out by flooding after the levees failed. Several patients were recovering from strokes or heart attacks suffered during the storm or the aftermath. One woman told me that on the day after the levees broke, she had been in the kitchen of a shelter on the West Bank, cooking jambalaya for volunteer rescuers, when she collapsed. "Next thing I know, I'm here," she said.

Another tiny, wrinkled woman I'll call Mrs. Theriot sat hunched in a wheelchair, and nurses told us she was ninety-five years old and the mother of eighteen children. Mrs. Theriot was lively and talkative, but she spoke only Cajun French. Thibodaux is deep in the southwestern section of Louisiana called Acadiana, the area settled by French Canadians chased from their home in the New World by the British in 1755 during the French and Indian War. The exiles came from Acadia, which encompassed parts of the Canadian Atlantic coast, primarily the areas now known as Nova Scotia, New Brunswick, and Prince Edward Island. Large numbers of the French-speaking Acadians settled along the bayous and coastline of southern Louisiana, bringing their language and culture with them.

Over time, these Acadian exiles mixed and married with earlier French settlers, German immigrants, Native Americans, French-speaking Creoles from the Caribbean islands, and others. Their descendants became a distinct ethnic group known as Cajuns. They kept their traditional rural occupations and values, as well as their French language, which over the years developed into a regional patois with several dialects, collectively known as "Cajun French." Although now somewhat Americanized, the Cajuns are still a unique people with a lively culture, and large numbers are still clustered in the small communities of Acadiana, including Thibodaux and its more populous neighbor, Lafayette. Music plays a big part in the Cajun culture, and we'd experienced their distinctive music and dancing during that special evening in Lafayette the previous October.

Mrs. Theriot had a steady stream of family members visit, all chattering in Cajun French. I enjoyed hearing their lilting cadences at mealtimes, though the rudimentary French I remembered from school bore almost no relation to their speech, and I couldn't understand a word.

"Do you understand any of that talk?" I asked Bob one afternoon as we gathered with other patients in the common room for lunch. "You're the French expert—remember Tinos?"

On our island-hopping trip to Greece in 1971, we had landed on Tinos during the strong summer winds Bob told me were called the *meltemi*.

"A gift of Aeolus, god of the winds," Bob had said. "Remember him in the *Odyssey*?"

"Oh yeah, something about winds and a bag, right?"

"Right. He gave Odysseus the bag of winds that powered his ship and got him home." Back then I was learning that being married to Bob was like having my own personal reference book.

The hotel on Tinos had no record of our reservations, and its proprietress, a tiny blonde woman with a chartreuse scarf wound around her neck, spoke only French. Later, she never appeared without trailing a shimmering scarf—she reminded us of the character Bobolina in *Zorba the Greek*. Her attitude was dismissive, until Bob dredged up enough French from his comparative literature studies to link the winds to Aeolus.

"Ah, Madame," said Bob in his most courtly tone. "Aeolus fait le vent souffler ce matin."

"Oui!" Her face broke into a delighted smile, and she gazed enraptured at the tall, Swedish-looking American, barely acknowledging the dark-haired young wife. "Aeolus, oui!"

Bob managed to ask for a room, and she agreed to put us in an outbuilding behind the hotel, chattering to Bob in rapid-fire French. He told me later he understood only about two thirds of it, but whenever we later encountered Madame, Bob would greet her with "Bonjour, Madame," mention the winds, and invoke Aeolus.

She would dissolve in giggles and *oui, oui, oui*'s, thoroughly charmed.

Now listening to the Theriot family, Bob said, "Tinos was a *long* time ago. Some of those words sound familiar, but it's not the French I remember. I have no idea what they're saying."

A number of the Thibodaux staff were Cajun themselves or spoke the language and could easily communicate with Mrs. Theriot. Talking to the rest of us, some of the staff spoke English with a few regional quirks, too. For example, they seemed to call everyone "Boo." When a nurse came in one morning with Bob's medicine and said, "Here're your pills, Boo," I asked her what the word meant.

"I don't know," she said. "I don't think it means anything. Don't you call people Boo?"

A couple in the room across the hall were conducting an agonized search for the two dogs they left behind in St. Bernard Parish. She was a small, sixty-ish woman with tinted blonde hair. She spoke in a high-pitched voice and called her gray-haired husband "Daddy." A thin but still-muscular man, he'd suffered a stroke soon after the storm and was trying to recover speech and movement on one side of his body, and he seemed to be making progress. Meanwhile, she searched the Internet's burgeoning "lost pets" web sites. One day, they were elated. Her husband's eyes were bright and a smile nudged the frozen muscles of his face as she told all of us they'd found one of their dogs in Arizona. Their elation turned to sorrow the next day when that dog turned out not to be theirs.

We all settled into a routine of communal meals, individual and group physical and occupational therapy for the patients, and more waiting. The hospital made computers available to us, and I was thrilled to find that the *Times-Picayune* was available in the lobby. Its New Orleans offices were underwater, but the newspaper had set up shop in Baton Rouge and resumed publication almost at once, giving all of us vital news of home. Televisions were tuned to constant coverage of the death and destruction in New Orleans and along the Gulf Coast.

In addition to survivors, rescuers now searched for bodies. Homes and stores in New Orleans continued to be broken into by scavengers desperate for food or looking for loot. The police and National Guard were overwhelmed. Finally, Lt. General Russel Honoré, commander of the 1st Army, a man Mayor Nagin called the "John Wayne Dude," landed in a helicopter, took charge, and slowly restored order. People who had stayed trapped in their homes, many because they feared leaving pets or possessions, now got orders to evacuate the city, even those parts that had not flooded. Meanwhile, refugees at the Superdome, Convention Center, and other areas of New Orleans had been bused at long last to shelters all over the country. Mayor Bill White of Houston was particularly welcoming, and thousands of evacuees streamed into Texas. Like us, New Orleans residents displaced by the deluge looked back at a city destroyed. None of us knew what the future would hold, though we were getting a sense that it would be a long time, if ever, before things were "normal" again.

When Katrina's chaser, Tropical Storm Rita, formed in the Atlantic and moved into the Gulf during the week of September 18, all of us in the Rehab Unit watched weather reports with a mixture of dread and disbelief. Gathering strength over the week, Rita became a powerful Category Five hurricane. It appeared to be headed for western Louisiana or Texas, but the cone of uncertainty was wide, and we knew from experience that a hurricane's path could change. If it followed predictions, Thibodaux could be on the eastern, more dangerous side of the winds. Another fearsome storm—yet the reaction on the Rehab floor was strangely muted, as if we were all numb and unable to take in the threat of a repeat experience.

We gazed at televised reports of the evacuation of Galveston, Lake Charles, Beaumont, and Houston. The exodus from Houston was plagued by long traffic jams, stalled cars, and chaos along major highways. One bus full of evacuees from a nursing home caught fire, killing its occupants, and there were stories of misery and other deaths along the clogged highways.

"At least New Orleans did one thing right," I said. "That 'contraflow' plan worked with Katrina."

"After the mess with Ivan," said Bob, "somebody learned some lessons." We'd been doing chemo in Houston in the summer of 2004, when Hurricane Ivan had threatened New Orleans. People were stuck in twelve-hour traffic jams leaving the city, then faced more delays trying to return when Ivan turned east and missed New Orleans.

Before Katrina hit, Louisiana's "contraflow" plan turned major highways into one-way evacuation arteries and got massive numbers of people out of New Orleans relatively efficiently. Now many who had found refuge in Texas were on the move again, fleeing Rita and stuck on Houston highways and along congested roads throughout southeastern Texas and western Louisiana.

One new patient arrived in Rehab that week, a very proper lady whose steel-gray hair was held back by tortoise shell combs. She wore embroidered bed jackets and looked the type to head a genteel garden club or book society. She had been evacuated from her home in the Garden District of New Orleans to stay with family in Galveston, where she'd suffered a minor stroke. Now with Rita approaching, her family had moved her from Galveston Island to Thibodaux. Over breakfast one day, as she struggled to manipulate her cutlery with stroke-stiff fingers, we speculated about when we'd be able to get back to our homes in New Orleans. She was the first to mention refrigerators.

"Just don't open the door, honey," she told me. "That's my advice. You won't want anything in that refrigerator."

Now the question on all our minds was how safe were we in this hospital? Would Rita threaten us here? Like Katrina, this new storm gained force as it moved through the Gulf of Mexico, and by the end of the week, Rita was an extremely dangerous hurricane with sustained winds of 165 miles per hour. The predicted landfall was still far to the west of us, but we heard staff from Thibodaux and surrounding towns talking about boarding up their homes and securing fishing camps and boats. On the map, I saw that we were less than fifty miles from the Gulf Coast and surrounded by lakes and bayous. Family members made frantic calls, wondering whether Bob and I should somehow try to evacuate Thibodaux. But although Bob was making progress and getting stronger daily, he was still weak, and we decided traveling wasn't a good idea—especially in view of the reports of terrible traffic delays.

Once again, we would have to ride out the storm and hope a hospital would keep us safe.

Early on Saturday morning, September 24, I walked out of the main doors, hoping to get to the supermarket about a hundred yards on the other side of the parking lot to pick up a few snacks before the storm hit. I wonder now what possessed me to go outside—I must have been in a daze. I managed to walk less than twenty feet when I was slammed by a fierce wind squall and almost blown over. Suddenly I felt like the manic Anderson Cooper, who had left New Orleans, where he had been broadcasting on CNN non-stop since Katrina, and moved to a coastal spot in Rita's path. For days we'd seen him on TV, with his staccato, hysterical weather warnings in front of the cameras, fighting to stay upright against the winds and waves. I gave up on getting to the market and retreated to the shelter of the lobby.

Feeling the blast from Rita's powerful winds cracked my cocoon of numbness, and the first stirrings of panic rattled me as I waited for the elevator to the Rehab floor. Did anyone really know where this hurricane would land? What if Rita hit close to Thibodaux? Could we survive another storm trapped in a hospital? What if this place lost power like Memorial? Could Bob endure more days of killing heat and helplessness? Were we close enough to the Gulf that tidal surges might engulf this building? Were we crazy to stay here? Was it too late to get out?

When I rushed to the Rehab nurses' desk, they tried to reassure me.

"Where are the hospital's emergency generators?" I asked. "Are they up high so they won't flood? What if we have to evacuate this building? Is there a plan?"

"Don't worry," said the nurse named Peggy. Her eyes narrowed and her tone was soothing, as if she recognized the signs of meltdown. "We've got generators, and they're safe."

"We've never had to evacuate this building, ever," said Carol, another nurse. "But if we do, we'll have plenty of warning, and we do have disaster plans. The building's solid, and the generators will work. We'll be okay."

"But the helipad is on the ground by the parking lot," I said. "What if it floods? My husband can't go through all that again." All the nurses had heard our story.

"They'll use ambulances. And this place won't flood." Carol moved to give my arm a reassuring squeeze. "Try to relax. We're in for a wild day, but we'll get through this storm."

"Really, it doesn't sound like it's coming here," said Peggy. "We'll be okay."

Easy for them to say, I thought. Staff at Memorial had thought we were safe, too. We shouldn't have stayed here. But I took a deep breath. "Okay," I said. "Let's hope you're right."

Returning to the room, I told Bob the winds had nearly blown me over. I hadn't made it to the market.

"Maybe we were wrong not to evacuate this time," I said, moving to look out the window.

Bob tried to calm me, too. "It sounds like it's going west, but better stay inside now. Not much we can do at this point but ride it out."

"The family asked last week if they should check on private helicopters or planes—I should've said yes."

"I'm not all that eager to get on another helicopter," said Bob. "Anyway, it's too late now. Too windy to fly, and being here's better than being on the road somewhere. We'll be okay."

The skies darkened, and we spent all day watching trees bend and lightning flash around the hospital. The lights and ventilation kept humming as rain swirled outside and lashed against the windows in sheets. The eerie roar of the winds reminded me of the long day in Memorial. With nothing to do but listen to the wailing of the wind, I missed the distraction of the children in Memorial's hallways—and I even missed those cartoonish choruses of *Beauty and the Beast*. For me, the lyrics will be forever associated with wind and water and upheaval: *Just a little change...just a little scared....*

Once Rita had spent her fury and the winds calmed, things slowly returned to normal in the Rehab Unit. We learned that Rita had made landfall near the Texas-Louisiana border, just as predicted. Though the winds had weakened somewhat, the storm came ashore as a strong Category Three hurricane. Another surge and heavy rains caused more levee breaches, so low-lying areas of New Orleans flooded again, but the city was spared major wind damage from Rita, and Galveston and Houston also escaped a direct hit. Thibodaux caught the outer bands of the storm and suffered some wind damage. Areas west and south of us were flooded by storm surges, and parts of Lafayette, Abbeville, and other small towns nearby had severe water damage. Lake Charles, near the Texas border, was hit hard. Some coastal communities were totally destroyed, and areas of Louisiana that had escaped the worst of Katrina now fell victim to Rita, whose winds and water surges battered the entire southern part of the state, especially the southwestern parishes, and damaged southeastern Texas as well.

The marshes and wetlands that long ago gave Louisiana protection against hurricane surges have been disappearing at an alarming rate in recent decades, due mainly to oil and gas drilling in the Gulf and dredging by the U. S. Corps of Engineers. Every hour, the coastline shrinks as wetlands the size of a football field are lost. In the months after Katrina and Rita, new efforts would be mounted to get funds to restore those vital Louisiana marshlands and prevent the kind of devastation that New Orleans and many coastal communities suffered from those storms. Later, the disastrous oil spill in the spring of 2010 would cause new damage to the state's fragile wetlands.

With Rita, once again it was the individual residents and first responders who were the heroes. Although this time government officials were quicker to call for evacuation, local firefighters, police, EMTs, and ordinary people in boats were the ones who got their neighbors out. Shelters, already full, made room for more evacuees.

Memorable photos showed herds of cattle from the *vacheries*, the cattle ranches of Acadiana, stranded and surrounded by water, their faces blank with surprise.

Chapter Nine

Unreal City

September 26

In the weeks after the levees broke, residents were forbidden to return to New Orleans, and many who had stayed through the storm and the flood were ordered out forcibly, some at gunpoint. Through most of September, New Orleans remained officially closed as the water slowly drained out of the city and the police and National Guard tried to gain control over the chaos.

When in history had an entire American city been closed and declared off limits to its citizens? Never in my memory. Mayor Nagin announced a re-opening of some of the least-damaged areas on September 19, but the advance of Rita reversed that plan, and Rita's surges re-flooded some neighborhoods and sent new water into others. Residents were being allowed to return to neighboring Jefferson Parish, which included the suburbs of Metairie, Kenner, and other flooded areas, but Orleans Parish remained closed for most of the month. However, beginning Monday, September 26, it was announced that business owners would be permitted to return to the French Quarter and Central Business District—but only during the day. A strict 6:00 p.m. curfew was in effect.

Bob's rehab was progressing well. He had worked hard with both physical and occupational therapists, and he had recovered enough strength that doctors in Thibodaux wanted to discharge him. They told us they'd give us whatever time we needed to make arrangements for a place to go. Since M. D. Anderson in Houston had no room, we decided to go to Dallas, where we would be near many of the Perry family and we had some medical contacts. To make the trip easy for Bob, his brother George was arranging for an ambulance to take us from Thibodaux to Dallas. My resourceful sisters, Rainy and Liz, had managed to find and furnish an apartment where we could stay, not an easy task now that Dallas was full of evacuees who had fled both Katrina and Rita. Bob could continue rehab with the help of home-health therapists, and we would consult a Dallas oncologist about further treatment.

Before we left, I wanted to make a quick trip back to New Orleans to check on our house and get our car, still sitting—we hoped—on the seventh level of Magnolia Garage, where I'd left it more than three weeks ago. I decided the opening on September 26 for businesses was a good time to try.

"I don't think you should go alone," Bob said. "I'll worry too much—you have no idea what you might face in the city." The media were still carrying reports of everything from toxic air to contaminated water to marauding outlaws still on the loose with guns. TV showed truckloads of National Guard soldiers patrolling the streets, rifles and bayonets at the ready.

"Rainy and Liz have offered to go with me," I said. "They're trying to book flights, and the three of us can drive in and make it back easily in a day." I didn't want to go alone, either. Provided I could talk my way past the checkpoints, I would need help facing the house and driving the car back. Rainy, a consultant in southern California, and Liz, a manager with the California Coastal Commission, had first tried to discourage me from returning to the city, but once they realized I was determined to go, they both arranged to take vacation time to come to help their beleaguered older sister. It was possible we wouldn't be allowed in, but it seemed worth a try.

Bob knew we'd need our car in Dallas, and he worried about leaving it parked at Memorial, now that the hospital was closed and empty. So he agreed to the plan, although I knew he wished he could go back with me himself, and he probably would be anxious even though I'd have my sisters with me. I didn't like leaving him, but I wanted to go now, while I was close enough to New Orleans to make the trip in one day—once we were in Dallas, getting back to New Orleans would be harder and take longer. Now I could go knowing Bob would be well cared for in the Rehab Unit, and there was no telling when the city would be "open" again.

We made preparations for the re-entry on Monday, September 26. Rainy and Liz had to change routes away from Houston and Dallas to avoid Rita, but they managed to get tickets on Sunday to Jackson, Mississippi. At the Jackson airport, they emerged from their flights only to be rushed to the basement to wait out a tornado threat. We all wondered, what next? Two hurricanes, and now a tornado. But the tornado skipped past the airport, and they were finally able to rent a car and get on the road to Thibodaux. Along the way, gas was hard to find, and roads were strewn with storm debris, but they finally pulled into Thibodaux on Sunday night.

Liz was behind the wheel of their rented SUV. The youngest of my three siblings—I'm oldest, then Rainy, then our brother Bill—Liz is a tall, sturdily-built brunette. An experienced camper, she had brought sleeping bags in case they had to bed down in the lobby of the hospital. Luckily, they wouldn't have to camp in the lobby—I'd been checking area motels every day, and a room at a Ramada magically opened up that Sunday night. Rainy climbed down from the passenger seat. About my height, with a thick mane of wavy, golden blonde hair, Rainy had spent most every spare minute in the past two weeks making phone calls from California to Dallas, trying to find and furnish an apartment for us. They were both dressed in jeans and lightweight cotton shirts, ready for work. Until I greeted them, I hadn't realized how isolated and alone I'd been.

My sisters had come prepared. They'd both had the tetanus shots the Centers for Disease Control was recommending for anyone entering the flooded city. And they'd brought equipment to arm us for a variety of risks: industrial-strength gas masks for toxic air, rubber boots to wade through muck, heavy-duty gloves to protect against contaminated surfaces, even flashlights and pepper spray in case the garage or our house had been invaded by squatters.

On Monday morning, after Rainy and Liz had a quick visit with Bob, we packed their rental car with all our gear, including our cell phones. We took bottled water and turkey poor boys purchased at the supermarket adjacent to the hospital, since nothing would be available in the city.

Now that the time had come to leave, I lingered by Bob's bed. He was being stoic about my going, but I could see the concern in his eyes. I bent down to give him a hug.

"You'll be careful, won't you?" he said, his hand on my arm. "Call me if you can."

"Don't worry, we'll be super careful. And back before dark. We can't stay past the curfew. Meanwhile, the nurses will cater to your every whim." That got a smile.

"I'll be fine," he said. "Good luck." Bob had become a popular patient in the Rehab Unit, I think because people liked his witty comments. He was undemanding, too, always expressing gratitude for anything done for him. And everyone felt pity for all of us New Orleans refugees.

I was armed with a letter from a Thibodaux hospital official saying I was returning for medical records (true) and a document identifying me as a business owner (also true—although the address of the small internet book business Bob started when he retired was officially in Pennsylvania, much of our inventory was in New Orleans). I'd had a tetanus booster in Memorial's ER after my injury on the stairs. My black eye had faded, but some magenta and yellow streaks remained, and nurses were amused when I stuck a band-aid strategically over my eyebrow where the stitches had been.

"Hey," I said, "maybe the National Guard will see the bandage and have pity. This eye might get us past the roadblocks."

They laughed. Sandy, a cheerful nurse with long dark hair who had tended to Bob so often that we felt especially fond of her, gave me an even bigger band-aid, for dramatic effect.

"Go for it, Boo," she said.

. . .

We set out mid-morning on the 65-mile drive east on Highway 90 to New Orleans. Crossing the Mississippi over the Huey P. Long Bridge into Jefferson Parish, I suggested we avoid Interstate 10, where I expected there would be many checkpoints. Instead, we took the two-lane River Road east along the levee toward New Orleans. Signs of damage from the storm and the flood were everywhere: trees and power lines down, shingles and slates blown from roofs and whole roofs blown off, fences and small sheds collapsed. Resting my bandaged eye against the window, I stared out at an entire landscape looking battered. We passed the Ochsner Foundation Clinic and Hospital, one of the few health facilities that didn't flood and was fully functioning. On our right, the grass-covered earthen levee that rose high and held back the mighty Mississippi looked just the same as it always had, though in places it was littered with storm debris.

At the Orleans Parish border, we encountered a short line of other vehicles stopped at a checkpoint, mainly trucks with contractors' logos on their sides but also a few cars. We watched as one car made a U-turn and drove past us in the opposite direction. Finally we pulled up and a National Guard soldier approached our car. I rolled down the back window by my seat behind Liz, who was driving, and let him get a full view of my wounded eye. He was a fresh-faced young man who looked about the age of the college freshmen Bob and I used to teach. I spoke with my official teacher-voice.

"Morning, officer," I said, "I'm a resident of the French Quarter and a business owner. My husband was evacuated from Memorial/Baptist Hospital. He's now in a hospital in Thibodaux. I need to get back to my house to get some of his medical records and our car." I offered him the letter from the hospital and one of Bob's business cards. All three of us held our breath, half expecting we'd be ordered to turn around and return to Thibodaux, mission unaccomplished.

He eyed us all, gave a cursory glance to the documents, said "Okay, drive carefully," and waved us through.

"Yessss," shouted Liz as she drove away.

"Maybe luck is with us," I said, rolling up the window.

We turned from River Road onto St. Charles Avenue where it intersects South Carrollton, in the Riverbend area. Would we see total destruction in this part of Uptown New Orleans? The news reports had made the damage sound widespread—destruction from the storm and flood, the looting, even the rescue workers' breaking down doors to check for bodies or pets.

The regal old live oaks still lined St. Charles Avenue, but some had been blown down, so there were big gaps where trees had been, and downed branches covered the streetcar tracks. Some of the ornate old iron light poles were bent or broken. Evidence of flooding was sporadic. Water lines showed on some houses but not on others, and yards were strewn with tree branches and storm debris. Messages warning off looters were painted on a few doors, and marks left by rescuers searching for survivors or animals appeared on homes in some blocks. Later I learned the rescuers' special code: they would spray paint on the front of each house a large X, noting in each of its quadrants the date of search, the identity of the group searching, the number of people or pets rescued, and the number of bodies found.

As we passed Audubon Park and Tulane and Loyola Universities, the front of the campuses looked undamaged. Later, I learned that both universities suffered extensive flooding and some wind damage, and neither was able to open for months. Their students, like those from other New Orleans universities, were scattered all over the country, along with so many Katrina victims.

The stately old homes lining St. Charles looked intact, standing like solid anchors on the strip of land parallel to the Mississippi, one of the few areas above the flood. The most striking thing was the silence. No sounds of traffic. No clack of streetcars on the old rails. No voices or music streaming out of corner sandwich shops or bars. It seemed incredibly strange to drive down St. Charles Avenue, one of New Orleans' busiest streets, and meet no other vehicle.

When we turned onto Napoleon Avenue, evidence of flooding became more dramatic as we neared Memorial Hospital: brown water lines climbed higher and higher on houses, and windows were broken and gaping. Front lawns and shrubs were brown and dead, and a layer of grey mud covered streets and yards. Approaching the intersection with Claiborne Avenue, we saw the familiar remains of Memorial/Baptist, now empty and abandoned—our next major hurdle. Would I be able to get our car out of the garage, and what would be left of it?

We drove to a side street near the entrance to Magnolia Garage. The hulking concrete building brought memories flooding back of those terrible days we were trapped. Now the whole hospital complex looked deserted. Newspaper reports from Tenet had said Memorial was closed, and a fence had been erected at the front of the building, but the complex was not yet totally fenced off. Would we be allowed inside? And if we did go in, what would we encounter?

A couple of guards stood sentinel, and the sight of them made us doubtful about our chances of getting in. Taking a deep breath, I walked over to a burly man wearing a florescent vest and a badge and told him my car was parked in the garage.

"You want to drive it out?" he said. "Fine. Go ahead."

"Okay, great," I said. "I also left a bag of medical papers on the roof and I want to get that."

The guard shook his head. "I can't give you permission to go up there."

Yet he didn't say explicitly that I couldn't, and all three of us got the impression he wouldn't stop me if I did —he just didn't want to know. It was a small sign of the New Orleans-style "live and let live" attitude, and reassuring.

Liz stayed with the SUV. Slipping lightweight dust masks around our necks, just in case, and donning gloves, Rainy and I walked into Magnolia Garage and up the circular ramp. When we reached the second level, we came to the spot where Bob and I and so many others spent that miserable night in the flooded garage. Now, the low concrete ceiling loomed over us, and sunlight barely penetrated the dark and dusty interior. The floor was littered with old pallets, dirty sheets, heaps of trash, and other detritus—a filthy scene.

"I can't believe you slept here," said Rainy.

I pointed to a wheelchair still sitting at the back of the ramp, one footrest dangling. "That's the wheelchair Bob sat in for two days," I said.

Rainy shook her head, a pained expression on her face. "Unbelievable," she said.

We kept walking and approached the seventh level, and I was almost afraid to look. Would the car be there? Would it still have tires and rims and other parts? We rounded the ramp, and up ahead I saw our silver Accord, right where I'd left it. One fender was scratched and a headlight broken, but when I opened the trunk, I found everything, including the laptop, untouched. What's more, I turned the key and discovered the tank was still three-fourths full. We had debated bringing a can of gasoline in case the car's tank had been emptied, but we were afraid we wouldn't be allowed into the city with a gas can. I hadn't thought about the battery, though. Would sitting for most of a month have drained it? No, the engine started at soon as I turned the key.

"Bless you, Honda," I said, letting the engine run a few minutes before turning it off and climbing out of the car.

My elation at finding the car gave me incentive to think about climbing up to the roof to look for the abandoned plastic bag. I was still annoyed that that bag of important papers had been snatched away. Irrational or not, I wanted to get it back.

"Did you get the impression he was telling us 'go if you want but I don't want to know'?" I asked my sister.

"Yeah," she said. "I don't think he'll stop us. And how will he know? He's seven flights below us."

"It's worth a try," I said. "Let's do it."

We walked up to level eight, where Bob and I and others spent so many hours waiting. Empty gurneys and abandoned chairs rested near the ramp, and the floor was strewn with trash: crushed water bottles, torn latex gloves, filthy paper padding and towels and old sheets. From there we climbed the ramp to the three steep flights of metal stairs leading to the open roof and heliport. Again I was struck by how impossible it seemed that patients in wheelchairs and sheet slings had been carried up these stairs. I could imagine what Bob's thoughts had been, feeling himself lifted by strangers who were sweating with exertion, knowing he was totally dependent on their strength and effort as he looked down from a height of at least a hundred feet above the surrounding waters. He must have wondered, what's going to happen to me? I can't do this. I don't want to do this. And where have they taken Carolyn? He must have been in pain. Did he gasp for air and have trouble breathing? Was that when his lung collapsed, during that difficult ascent up these impossibly steep stairs?

When Rainy and I got to the roof, it was ankle-deep in trash. I started toward the tunnel but she grabbed my arm.

"Are you sure you want to walk through all this?" Rainy said, a grimace on her face.

"It's not far, just over there." I pointed. "We're up here now. I can't leave without looking."

So avoiding a few wires we feared might be live, we picked our way over mounds of empty plastic water bottles, old mattresses, abandoned pillows, even empty baby incubators, the kind where premature infants are kept. Several of these incubators were strewn about, and I pictured the frantic scene when tiny newborns were taken out of them and carried onto helicopters, bound for the unknown—without their mothers.

Entering the catwalk tunnel leading to the heliport, I stood at the spot where I remembered begging for my plastic bag and tote. I scanned the trash-strewn floor. Stuck against one side of the tunnel, torn and filthy amidst all the trash, I recognized my white plastic bag with the turquoise logo of Memorial Medical Center on the side. I rushed over to lift it from the floor. The papers inside were soggy but intact.

"I didn't tell you, but I had a dream that I came back and the bag was here," I said to Rainy. A few days ago, in the chair by Bob's bed in the Thibodaux hospital, I'd awakened from a dream of this tunnel I'd passed through in such a rush on the first day of September. The dream left me with a vivid image of the white plastic sack lying on the tunnel's floor. Still, it hardly seemed possible I'd found it. With all my other worries, at least I no longer had to worry about replacing these essential records.

On the way back down, the amazing find made me hopeful. "I wonder if there's any chance we could get the file box I left inside the hospital." Enough of our financial history was in that box to make an identity thief's job easy.

"You're not thinking of trying to go inside that building, are you?" asked Rainy. "No telling what germs are living in there. I don't think you should."

"No, I'm sure they wouldn't let me in," I said. "And I don't want to go. But they must be patrolling inside, and maybe I could get somebody to look for me. Seems like it's worth a try."

We returned to the car and drove it down the circular ramp, parking it on Magnolia Street near Liz's rental car. A second security guard had come out of the building and was standing across the street. He was a muscular man with a fresh-faced, genial smile, wearing an orange vest over tee shirt and shorts, a white dust mask hanging from an elastic band around his neck. I walked over to him and told him my story, describing the portable plastic file box I'd left on the third floor. He listened dubiously.

"You know where the box is?" he asked.

"On three, in a staff room near room 3158 in Clara Wing," I said. "Is there any chance you might see if you can find it?"

He was about to go on lunch break, but he said after lunch he would go inside and look. As he walked off, we debated. Should we spend time waiting or forget the files and go on to the house? My obsessive gene kicked in, and I decided this was probably my only opportunity to get that box back. Even if the chances of finding it seemed slim, I wanted to try. So we waited.

We sat on a concrete stoop and looked across at the front of Magnolia Garage. Rainy spotted the brown water line nearly ten feet up the building's façade.

"You mean the water got that high?" she said.

It dawned on us all that a layer of dried mud and flood detritus covered the concrete we were sitting on. "I don't think we should sit in this stuff," Liz said. We all got up, but we kept waiting.

About a half hour later, we saw the guard cross the street. He waved at us, then walked into the hospital building, wearing the mask and gloves. I thought about my own trip through those darkened hallways the night my escorts and I had found the room where Nurse Carolyn had stored my stuff. After more than three weeks of the late summer heat and humidity, with its clogged plumbing and airless spaces, the atmosphere in that building must have become unspeakably foul. I imagined the guard climbing the stairs to the third floor and moving down the hot, fetid hallway of Clara Wing.

It's there, I thought. Find that room. Find that box.

The three of us stared at the building for at least twenty minutes. Suddenly, I noticed movement. We looked up, and out of an open window three floors above the ground, its glass missing, hands thrust a square beige box. Then, moving from behind the box to the left side of the window, the inquiring face of the guard looked down at us, eyebrows raised.

"That's it," I yelled, my arms in the air as if to signal *touchdown*. Rainy and Liz and I sent up a cheer.

Still chattering about our amazing success, with Liz following us in the rental car, Rainy and I drove back down Napoleon, turned left on St. Charles Avenue, and drove through the Garden District toward the Central Business District. As we passed Josephine Street, I pointed to the left.

"Bob and I lived in an apartment in that building while our house was being renovated," I told Rainy. "We were right on the streetcar line." The place looked undamaged, but dark and forlorn.

Heading downtown, we encountered more and more signs of destruction caused by wind and especially water. Brown water lines stained the fronts of buildings in the downtown area. Windows were broken or still boarded up, and the florescent markings spray-painted by rescuers looked stark on the old buildings, noting dates of searches and numbers of bodies or pets found. We drove slowly, stopping at each main intersection. No signals worked, and although there was no other traffic, a slow pace seemed somehow fitting.

As we crossed Canal Street, the main boulevard at the upper edge of the French Quarter, we saw the large trailers, festooned with antennae, that were being used as bases for the journalists covering the disaster. They lined the neutral ground in the center of the boulevard. Many of the huge palm trees that had only recently been planted along Canal Street were blown over. Heaps of trash lined the sidewalks.

We drove into the Quarter itself, and here things began to look more intact. A few businesses seemed open. People emerged from doors carrying armloads of trash, adding it to the piles of debris in front of buildings. We passed jeeps and open trucks filled with soldiers in various uniforms. The Quarter looked far from normal, but there were signs of life.

"For the first time in memory, it's going to be easy to find a parking space on my street," I said to my sister. The street was deserted, and we were able to park both our cars directly in front of our house. We scanned the façade.

"Well, nothing looks damaged or disturbed," said Liz. Back home in California, she and Rainy had read newspaper accounts of looters and squatters moving into empty homes in the city, and they both had canisters of pepper spray in their hands as we emerged from the cars and crossed the street.

I put my key into the gate's lock, but before I turned it the gate swung open. Probably the gas company had forced the lock in order to turn off the main. A slight annoyance—they had a key. Why did they have to break in? We walked into the side courtyard, and from the outside, the house looked fine. When I opened the side door, however, all three of us gasped. The stench was like nothing I'd ever experienced—a thick, fetid odor of decay, overpowering. I quickly pulled the door shut.

"We're gonna need those masks," Rainy said. We went back to the car to get the three heavy-duty respirators, rubber gloves, and rubber boots to cover our sneakers. Armed, we returned to the door and made our way anxiously to the kitchen in the back of the house.

My eyes were drawn first to the window. It seemed to be covered with a black screen—hundreds of black flies. Clusters of flies also clung to the door of the refrigerator. On the hardwood floor, a large, dark puddle of liquid pooled under the refrigerator.

"Oh, Carolyn," Rainy said. "Water's on your poor hardwood floor."

Then the puddle moved, a slow undulation. "What is that?" I asked in horror.

"Maggots," said Liz. A pool of squirming maggots.

All three of us stared wide-eyed, fighting the instinct to flee. I had to rescue my heart pine floor. Armed with a broom, dustpan, bug spray and disinfectant, we made an assault on the maggots and the flies. I remembered the Garden District lady's warning not to open the refrigerator —everything in it had been marinating in 100-plus degree heat for three weeks.

"We've got to move the fridge out to the courtyard, but we can't open its door," I said. "I'll see if I can borrow a dolly."

I walked to the corner grocery. I'd seen an announcement on one of the "news of the Quarter" blogs that the Matassas were readying their store for reopening. It wasn't open yet, but today John and Louis Matassa were there, still cleaning out their own refrigeration units, and they loaned me a dolly and told me how to disconnect the water supply to the ice maker. I wheeled the dolly back to my kitchen, and the three of us wrestled the refrigerator out from the wall. The electricity was on again in this part of the city, so we pulled the plug from the wall outlet and tried to ease the refrigerator onto the dolly. But our feet slipped on the remains of the maggots, and we couldn't get purchase or leverage.

I opened the back French doors, walked down the three steps, and stood outside, my arms raised. "Here," I said. "You guys tip it over and I'll catch it from here."

My sisters stared at me for a long, silent moment. Later, they told me that's when they feared I was finally becoming unhinged.

"Carolyn, no, are you crazy? There's no way you can handle this packed fridge. It's too heavy. It'll fall on top of you," said Rainy. "Even three of us aren't strong enough."

"We'll have to open up its door," said Liz. "Let's empty it out. Uggghh."

"No, wait," I said. "Let me see if I can get some help. Maybe I can find a National Guard soldier who will help us move it. I'll go look." It was an excuse to get outside and away from the stench. Later, my sisters teased me, saying I'd deserted and left them to do the dirty work. They were right.

I got in my car and slowly drove up and down streets of the neighborhood, looking for a likely helper. In the blazing sun of the late September afternoon, people were busy carrying out armloads of trash from open storefronts, or removing sheets of plywood from windows. An odor of rot hung in the air. Heaps of debris lined every block, but the streets normally clogged with parked cars, traffic, and mule-drawn buggies carrying tourists were almost deserted, except for military vehicles. I spotted an open Humvee parked on lower Bourbon Street with six soldiers dressed in camouflage sitting in it. I parked behind them and approached.

"Hello," I said. "Could any of you possibly help me move my refrigerator out the door of my house?"

"Sorry, lady," one answered. "We're on a mission."

After cruising awhile with no luck, I returned to the house. My stalwart sisters had opened the fridge's door. Bulky respirators covered their faces, making them look like twin-snouted anteaters, and they were filling black garbage bags with what remained of the food I'd left behind. A turkey in the freezer, still in its plastic casing, had turned to amber liquid. The ham I'd left in the refrigerator section was unrecognizable, covered in maggots. Recoiling, I steeled myself and joined the effort.

Sweat poured down our foreheads. Rainy worked like a woman driven: thick hair pulled into a ponytail, perspiration ran down her face in rivulets as she scooped out handfuls of muck and stuffed it in bags that Liz held open. Their eyes above the respirators looked disbelieving. I'm not sure how many garbage bags we filled and stacked on the curb. Rainy said twenty.

Finally, working feverishly to finish and get out before the 6:00 p.m. curfew, we wrestled the empty refrigerator out the back doors, down three steps, and onto its side in the courtyard. It would stay there until I could return months later and pay two young men to move it to curbside, where it would join the legions of abandoned refrigerators lining the streets of New Orleans. Before leaving the courtyard, I checked the pond, looking for the goldfish I'd left swimming there on August 28. They were gone, blown away by Katrina.

Unfortunately, many of the fish housed in the Audubon Aquarium shared the same fate. Bob's prediction that the aquarium would withstand the storm was only partly true. The building stood on high ground near the river, so it didn't flood, but the structure suffered severe roof damage from the hurricane's winds. Withstanding the broken levees was another story. When power was lost for days during the flood, back-up generators were in place, but a clogged fuel line shut down the delicate life-support systems needed to oxygenate and clean the water. Staff who had been forced to evacuate returned later to find thousands of fish dead. The colony of penguins and Buck and Emma, the beloved sea otters, survived and were flown to the aquarium in Monterey Bay, California, and the giant sea turtle was sent to a facility on Galveston Island. Clownfish, seahorses and sea dragons went to the Dallas aquarium, and the Houston Zoo became a shelter for macaws and other birds. The white alligator and some surviving tarpon stayed in aquarium tanks while Audubon staff struggled to recover, and they managed to save hundreds of freshwater and saltwater fish. But as a result of the days without power, more than 4000 of the Audubon Aquarium's prized collection of fish died.

Thinking about the fish made me wonder about our neighbor's cat, Marie. Our neighbor Bill had been out of town during the week before the storm, and a sitter came daily to feed his cat. I hoped the sitter had managed to evacuate Marie. Later, I learned that Marie had been one of those who rode out the storm at home. When Bill was able to send the animal rescuers into his house in the weeks following the storm to check on the cat, they found, scattered throughout the house and interior courtyard, loose feathers and the remains of a sparrow. Marie had fended for herself, and was fine.

Not all pets were so lucky. Later we learned that Bosco, our friend Steve's injured German shepherd, didn't survive the long evacuation trip to Dallas. He died en route, less than an hour away from the surgery that might have saved him. I never learned for certain the fate of the animals trapped with us in the Memorial garage. I read that some owners, rather than abandon their dogs and cats, begged doctors to euthanize the animals, and that a few of the staff who stayed until the end of the evacuation were finally allowed to bring their pets onto boats with them. I hope the ER doctor and nurse's Irish setter was one of those. But most of the Magnolia pets had to be abandoned, their owners forced to leave them with little food or water in the sweltering heat. In the weeks following the storm, it became clear that many of the people who drowned in the city had stayed because they refused to evacuate without their pets. Others were forced to make that terrible decision to desert creatures that were totally dependent on them. By conservative estimates, over 50,000 animals were left behind in the flooded city. Animal rescuers streamed into New Orleans after the waters receded and managed to deliver some to shelters all over the country, where they were sometimes reunited with their searching owners. But in addition to more than two thousand humans dead or missing in New Orleans and all over the Gulf Coast, thousands of animals perished.

Now I stood over the empty fish pond, staring at the murky water while Rainy and Liz began packing the cars. Finally, only minutes ahead of the curfew, I closed and bolted the back doors and shutters and took a last look at the rooms of the small house, wondering how long it would be before Bob and I could come back home. I closed the door, locked the gate, and with Rainy following in the rental SUV, Liz and I drove slowly out of the French Quarter. Although spared the ravages of floodwater, the old historic district had suffered from the winds. Slates from roofs littered the streets and sidewalks. On Royal Street, the garden behind St. Louis Cathedral had lost some of its majestic old magnolia trees, and the normally ordered plants were a jumbled mess. But the French Quarter, the original settlement of New Orleans, had survived many hurricanes, and the quirky neighborhood was slowly coming back to life. As we turned onto St. Louis Street, we encountered an impromptu street party: people sat on the sidewalk at two white-clothed tables, each with a silver champagne bucket, raising flutes to toast passersby as music floated from the Kelsto Club, a nearby bar.

I phoned Bob from the car and told him the good news that our house had only minor wind damage, inside and out. I had taken pictures of some fallen roof slates and cracks in interior ceilings and walls. I could hear the surprise in his voice at the unexpected news that I'd been back to Memorial and retrieved all our stuff.

"You found the file box, too?" he said. "Amazing."

"But our refrigerator's in the courtyard," I said.

"What?" Bob said. "In the courtyard? Why?"

Bob and I had shopped for a long time for that refrigerator. It was the first we'd had with an automatic ice maker. Bob's glee when he watched those magic cubes effortlessly appear, ready to be plunked into highball glasses, was contagious. He loved that appliance.

"Trust me," I said. "You would never want anything from that fridge, ever again."

The smell of decay had permeated our clothes, and we rode with windows open. It would be weeks before the lingering stench in the car dissipated. Our route out of town took us up South Claiborne Avenue toward Jefferson Highway and the Huey P. Long Bridge. All along the Claiborne neutral ground, the carcasses of flooded cars, trucks, and boats sat helter skelter where the receding waters had left them, some resting at odd angles and all covered with grey, dried mud. We passed again the hulking wreck of Memorial Hospital, broken windows gaping.

Still hanging from one window was a hand-lettered sign, begging "Please Help."

The white convertible, seen from hospital room Monday, Aug. 29, 2005.

Front of Magnolia Garage with heliport on top.

Hospital window smashed by chair on Aug. 31, 2005.

8th level of garage, where patients waited all day Aug. 31.

Scene on garage level 2 where patients spent the night of August 31.

Evacuation route: steep stairs and tunnel leading to helipad on roof.

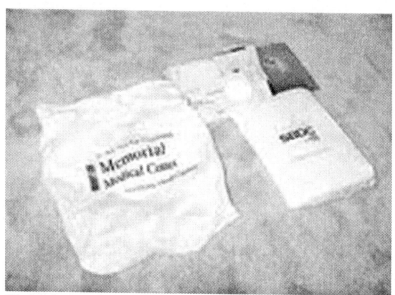

Plastic bag and contents recovered from Magnolia roof Sept. 26, 2005.

Chapter Ten

That Stone Wall

September 29 – November 9

The ambulance pulled up on a sunny Thursday morning. Staff from the Thibodaux Medical Center helped Bob out of his wheelchair and onto a gurney where he would ride for the eight-hour trip to Dallas. In a few short weeks, Thibodaux had become a familiar haven, and in a way, we were both reluctant to leave. Later, Bob said to me, "I should've stayed in Thibodaux. I felt safe there." But the cheerful driver from Acadian Ambulance Service got Bob settled then told me he would follow me to the Lafayette airport, where I could return the rental Chevy. A paramedic sat in the back of the ambulance to keep watch over Bob. Two nurses and a social worker waved as we drove off.

Bob's work over the previous month with occupational therapists had strengthened his muscles and prepared him to be a passenger in our car, but Bob's brother George made arrangements for the private ambulance that would spare both of us the long drive, and after our quick trip back to New Orleans to retrieve our car the previous Monday, my sisters had driven it and their rented SUV to Dallas. They'd be waiting there in the furnished apartment where Bob and I would spend an uncertain number of weeks or months, part of what was being called the Katrina Diaspora.

When I emerged from the Lafayette terminal, the Acadian driver was waiting and directed me into the front passenger seat. The five-hundred-mile trip in the ambulance passed in a blur. Traveling north, we followed roughly the path that Hurricane Rita had taken less than a week before. Downed trees, flattened fences, and battered structures, many roofless or covered by the ubiquitous blue FEMA tarps, dotted the landscape. Brown water from heavy rain, overflowing streams, or flooded bayous stood stagnant in pools bordering the highway. Billboards were flattened or broken. From my shotgun seat high in the ambulance, I looked out over occasional fields of cotton, and field after field of soybeans, mowed down by Rita's winds.

The driver kept a steady speed, questioning me about our Katrina experience and telling stories of his exploits rescuing people before and after Rita. I turned back periodically to check on Bob. He was stretched out flat on the gurney, wearing shorts and a tee-shirt, covered by a light blanket, with a blood pressure band around his arm. I could talk to him through the partition that separated the back of the ambulance, but we had to shout over the road noise, so conversation wasn't easy.

"How're you doing, hon?" I called out at one point.

"Cold," he said.

"Sorry, this is the only blanket we have," said the paramedic in back with Bob.

The driver frowned. "There's a town coming up. We'll look for a store where you can find him a cover."

Before long, he pulled into a Dollar store not far from the highway. I climbed down from the high passenger seat, went inside, and emerged with a fluffy cotton quilt that would give Bob more protection against the air conditioning. Customers going in and out of the store gave us curious glances but continued on their way, as if an ambulance parked at a Dollar store was just one more strange sight in the post-hurricane landscape.

On the outskirts of Shreveport, the ambulance slowed again.

"Better get gas for the beast," said the driver. "Keep your eye out for a station that sells diesel."

In the past week, residents fleeing Rita and then returning after the storm had clogged the highways throughout western Louisiana and eastern Texas, creating periodic gridlock and gas shortages, and interruptions at refineries meant supplies were low. We passed several stations with signs proclaiming "NO GAS."

"There's a diesel sign," I said finally. Cars were waiting in line at two pumps for regular gas, but when the driver pulled our ambulance around back to the diesel pump, we found the nozzle chained under a handwritten sign saying simply, "Out."

Several large eighteen-wheelers were parked at the back of the lot. Leaning on the side of his truck, one driver called out to us, "Diesel be here in a hour, they say. Supply trucks coming."

Our driver waved to him but said to me, "Let's keep looking. We got awhile before we're out."

Great, I thought. Just what we need. Stranded on a nowhere highway in an ambulance out of gas. But all I said was, "Okay. I hope we find some."

The driver shifted into reverse and deftly maneuvered the big ambulance back and away from the empty diesel pump. Driving in reverse had once posed a huge problem for Bob and me. On a holiday trip to the island of Crete, we'd rented a tiny 1978 Opel hatchback, with a feature that was then new to us: a sun roof. We drove it happily out of the rental lot, looking forward to cruising around the sunny island with the roof open to the Greek sky. We parked the car in our hotel lot and didn't discover the problem until the next day. Neither of us could figure out how to put the car in reverse. It had a manual transmission, as most European cars did in those days, and we moved the stick shift to every position possible, to no avail. The car wouldn't back up.

"You drive," said Bob. "Put it in neutral, and I'll push." Bob stood in front of the small car, gave it a push, and the Opel moved backward out of the parking space. Then he jumped in and we set off, moving forward as Cretan passers-by watched with bemused looks.

Returning to the airport meant backtracking some distance and losing time, and neither of us knew enough Greek to explain the problem to an agent over the phone. Besides, it was Christmas Eve and the office would probably be closed. So for most of our week on Crete, we handled reverse the same way: contriving to park in ways that wouldn't require backing up, and when we had to, applying the neutral/push method and trying to ignore the amused reactions of onlookers. Only near the end of our trip did we learn from a helpful gas station attendant that it took a simple push downward on the gear shift to make it easily move to the reverse position.

Dusk had fallen as the ambulance driver now eased into traffic on Interstate 20. West of Shreveport, just over the Texas border, we finally spotted a large station where a long line of trucks snaked up to two working diesel pumps. The attendants waved our ambulance to the front of the line, and we were soon back on the road, tank full.

It was almost ten o'clock when the ambulance finally pulled up in front of a small, ground floor apartment off Shady Brook Lane in Dallas. The driver and paramedic helped Bob inside then carried his rented wheelchair and our small bag into the apartment. My sisters had rented furniture, and Perry family members had stocked the kitchen. The next day, Rainy and Liz flew home to California, and Bob and I settled in for an extended stay in yet another new place.

In those October weeks, Bob continued to fight. He worked with therapists who came regularly to the apartment, trying to maintain and increase the strength he'd gained in rehab at Thibodaux. Visits from family cheered him. Bob's brother and sisters-in-law, his nephews, grandnephews and nieces and their wives and husbands all lived nearby. My sisters came again from California, my brother flew in from Raleigh, and his son Simon, our godson, traveled from his college campus in New York. All the family embraced us with warmth and caring, and Bob made enormous efforts to be as close to his old self as he could for them. He dressed and came to the table for meals. He accepted help when he needed it. He seldom complained, but Bob had an independent streak, and he'd always taken great care with his health and appearance. He'd been tall and fit, and proud of his physique. Now his muscle tone was withering, and his shoulders began to stoop from sitting hunched in the wheelchair. His weight kept dropping, and he needed help with basic functions of daily life.

One night he said to me, "My body's betraying me."

Sister-in-law Nell came to the apartment on a day in early October, not long after we'd arrived in Dallas, the first time she'd seen Bob since his treatment began. She must have been startled at his appearance, but she greeted him with a hug. "You're looking just as handsome as ever."

"Thank you for that," he said with a half-smile. His tone was rueful.

Occasionally, I saw a flash of anger. When that happened, I usually tried to soothe or ignore it, or even cater to the anger. But by the time we got to Dallas, my nerves were frayed too, and I reacted one night when, as he tried to position his wheelchair at the table for dinner, his mouth in a grim line, Bob snapped at me when I asked if he wanted some vegetable soup.

"No," he growled. "It looks vile. I wish you'd stop trying to make me eat."

Stung, I said, "Now I know how those caregivers feel when their patient turns mean."

Bob reacted instantly. "I'm sorry," he said. "That's not me. You know I'm not really like that."

"I know, of course I know." I jumped up and hugged him, pierced with regret at what I'd said. "You're brave and good and you've never been mean, and I love you." I had been awed at the way Bob faced this cancer. Never a very patient man, he submitted with courage and grace to month after month of debilitating treatments and grim side effects—his poor body was ravaged from the constant barrage of toxic chemicals. He groused at times and had moments of self-pity and anger, but they never lasted long. He took care to thank me often for the help I gave him, and he did everything he could to lessen the burden of his illness on me. Years before, he'd been the one who cared for me after I had back surgery and had to wear a brace for months. Every day, cheerfully and without being asked, he had helped me to bathe. Seeing him now, his body diminished and his hopes dashed, was almost more than I could bear.

He never lost his special sense of humor. One day, he didn't have strength enough to push himself out of a huge, deep-cushioned recliner in the apartment. He announced, "Houston, we have a problem."

I tried to help him stand, but even together we couldn't do it. Bob's grandnephew Travis and his wife lived nearby and came to the rescue, and as they walked in the door, Bob greeted them with a cheery, "Fancy meeting you here. Pardon me if I don't get up."

Later, I got him a chair with an automatic lift. He'd press the lever to activate the seat and intone, "Countdown to launch: ten, nine, eight..." as the chair raised him slowly up. Every time, the sight made me giggle.

One Sunday evening six of us gathered in our apartment for a pizza dinner: Nell, nephew Randy and his wife Suzzi, Bob and I, my sister Liz. I pulled out a video camera and panned the group around the table, urging everyone to "say something." In the past, Bob had teased me about my attempts to record such events, sometimes calling me "Brenda Starr, Girl Reporter," a reference to that old comic strip character, and this time he stayed true to form. When the camera got to Bob, sitting quietly in his wheelchair with a bottle of Boost in front of him, we all laughed at his wry commentary spoken in that resonant voice: "This is Family Moment Number Thirty."

Was Bob thinking about death during those weeks? Of course he must have been, but I don't think he expected it soon. About six weeks before Katrina hit New Orleans, we'd been propped next to each other in bed, sipping coffee and talking as we did most mornings. Suddenly out of the blue, Bob mentioned a piece of property we'd bought before his retirement, when we thought we'd spend summers back in Pennsylvania.

"We should go ahead and build that house on the ridge," he said. "I think I'll be around to enjoy it, at least for awhile." That was in mid-July.

Later, after the ordeal in Memorial, when the doctor in Thibodaux wouldn't resume chemotherapy and when an oncologist we consulted in Dallas agreed that he was still too weak for more chemo, Bob surely knew the cancer was advancing, but even then he didn't talk about dying. As the weeks passed into autumn and the leaves on the oak tree outside the window by his chair turned russet and then brown, did he start believing he was nearing the end? Was he moving toward the acceptance psychologists say is the final stage? If so, he never talked about it. I wonder now if he thought about what Tennessee Williams wrote in his *Notebooks* about death: "Last night the thought of death disturbed me greatly. Tonight I view it very objectively like a stone wall at the other end of the road—of course, I'm in no hurry to reach it."

Looking back, I think Bob did pass through those classic phases identified by Elizabeth Kubler-Ross, though for him the stages didn't occur in a linear sequence. Bargaining came first, I think, and was part of the process of chemotherapy and the accompanying treatments. I saw only a few signs of denial. One occurred during the short remission, when he had thought the treatment was successful. When jaundice began to give his skin a yellow tinge and other symptoms reappeared, he refused for a time to acknowledge them, insisting the yellow skin was my imagination. After he had submitted to another cycle of chemotherapy, this one more harsh and difficult, he did alternate for a time between anger and depression. Often during chemo he stubbornly neglected to drink the large quantities of water he knew he should, and he got angry when I reminded him. He spent a lot more time in his favorite soft-leather chair, but often napping instead of reading as he used to do. In early August, he told the doctor, "I think I'm a little depressed." Dr. Veith replied it would be surprising if he weren't.

Bob's personality was complex, and I don't think it fit those rigid five stages. It was more like him to try deliberately *not* to fit them. We paid constant attention to his physical condition, but as the disease progressed in those autumn weeks, we seldom discussed what he was thinking or feeling. We, who both were trained in analysis and discourse, whose lives had been built around words, faced this ultimate topic with silence.

I must have known on some deep level that I was watching Bob approach that stone wall, but I was still intent on fighting, still urging him to build his strength, still insisting we'd find some drug that would work. I didn't want to lose him, so I refused to believe I would. From the start, we both had been convinced he would survive—after all, he'd beat cancer twice before.

There had been times when fear reared up. During the first chemo cycle, one night when he felt particularly low, Bob asked me in a wistful voice, "Do you really think I'll see Windermere again?" That lake in England had become for us a special place of peace and beauty, a refuge, a goal.

"Yes," was my adamant answer. "I know you will. As soon as you're well again, we'll go back—that'll be our first trip." A shiver of fear shot through me, but I pushed it back.

Bob had once called me "Pollyanna" and maybe I was, but the almost palpable sense of hope that pervaded the hallways and waiting rooms of the M. D. Anderson clinic had made believers of us both: we watched the television ads celebrating survivors of all types of cancer, we read the success stories, we gazed at the colorful fish darting through turquoise tanks and kept that positive attitude everyone said was so important. The people we encountered—doctors, nurses, fellow patients, spouses and families—seemed totally focused on hope. Discussing chemotherapy, oncologists mentioned the possibility that the cancer would "stop responding," but there always seemed to be an alternative drug or therapy waiting in the wings if that happened.

A social worker helped us fill out forms to ensure power of attorney for health decisions, a clear acknowledgment that the patient might not be able to make decisions at some point, but that point was never dwelt on. I signed the forms, but for me, needing them seemed far in the future. It is said that a dying person's loved ones go through those same psychological stages. I certainly had my share of anger—though most of it came later—and I definitely tried some bargaining, but my overwhelming response throughout those months was denial.

I called it hope.

That must have been why I reacted so negatively to all mention of hospice. I knew and approved of the basic philosophy of hospice: trying to provide a comfortable, dignified death. I just wasn't ready to apply it to us. I thought hospice meant the end of treatment, the end of hope. Does the instinct to fight for survival hang on past all reason? For me it did.

Near the end of October, symptoms of jaundice returned. Although therapists still came to the apartment, Bob's sessions got shorter, and twice he asked me to cancel their visits altogether. Five days before Halloween, as a pumpkin I'd carved to amuse him grinned on the patio outside his window, Bob pushed the lever to raise himself from the recliner. Upright for a moment, he silently collapsed to the floor. I rushed to help him, but he was too weak to stand. An ambulance took him to Baylor Hospital's ER.

In the emergency room, I focused on treatment. From the color of his complexion and other symptoms, I knew a gastrointestinal stent placed in July was blocked and needed to be replaced. I insisted on the procedure, and the ER doctor agreed to arrange it, to make Bob "more comfortable." Then he asked if Bob had a "Do Not Resuscitate" order.

I shook my head and gave the same answer I always had: "No. But I have his signed Power of Attorney for Health." Many times over our years together, Bob and I had discussed end-of-life decisions, but always in the abstract. We agreed neither of us wanted to be kept alive by machines when there was no hope of recovery. But facing the reality—actually grasping that hope was gone—that was the tricky part. That I hadn't done. The doctor turned and addressed Bob directly.

"Mr. Perry, if your heart stops in the course of treatment, do you want us to shock you and try to start it artificially?"

"No," Bob replied, his voice strong and loud.

"Bob, wait," I said. "Are you sure?" I was shocked. I'd never heard him say that.

The doctor glared at me. "We have to respect the patient's wishes," he said, emphasizing the word *patient* and making a note in Bob's chart.

I let it pass, intent on getting Bob's symptoms relieved and getting him into a room. In the week that followed, Bob was treated by the palliative care team, who again urged us to consider hospice. They sensed I was the one resisting, and they gently tried to educate me about what hospice offered. When hospice advocates came to talk to me, I kept asking, "What happens if Bob rallies and gets stronger, and wants to start the new chemo?"

Representatives from some of the hospice organizations answered patiently that if that happened, resuming treatment was an option he could choose. That answer satisfied me. On November 4, we agreed to sign the papers admitting Bob to a hospice program. No one—not the hospice staff, not the palliative care team, not any of the doctors—ever said to me, "That's not going to happen. Your husband is not going to get better."

Maybe they thought it was obvious. They all dealt with me as an intelligent person. No one ignored or condescended to me. They tried to overcome my resistance to their vision of what we should do. Yet none of them grasped the depth of my denial. None of them said, "Wake up. Look at Bob. He's going to die and it's likely to be soon."

Everybody said I behaved so well. During the ten days we spent in that hospital, I was with him by day and slept by his bed at night. I coordinated visits of family members, who came in a steady stream to visit their brother, their brother-in-law, their Uncle Bob. We all did our best to surround him with love. He responded by being himself, thanking everyone for coming and even managing to joke that grandnephew Matt was "looking portly." When another grandnephew talked at length to Bob, telling him about some recent adventure, Bob seemed to nod off to sleep, but as Taylor ended and rose to leave, Bob said quietly, "Thank you for that story, Taylor."

I watched over and talked to Bob too, and tried to interpret every want or need. In the background, I played upbeat New Orleans music to cheer him: Pete Fountain's clarinet, Kermit Ruffins' trumpet, the piano of Dr. John. One day, I even danced a little to "China Boy," one of his favorites. Watching me from the bed, he smiled.

Yet even when Bob needed help rolling over, when he stopped taking anything but fruit juice or Boost, when he slept nearly all the time and our conversation was limited mostly to my "Would you like a sip of water?" and his quiet "Yes, please"—even then, I didn't realize how close death was. Perhaps if he had wanted to talk, he would have, but I didn't try to talk to him about what he was feeling. Was he trying to spare me? I wonder now if that couplet from Shakespeare's Sonnet Sixty-six about "restful death" crossed his mind: "Tired with all these, from these would I be gone,/ Save that, to die, I leave my love alone."

For months, any pain Bob had was successfully controlled with drugs like Tylenol or Darvon. On the Saturday night nine days after he was admitted to the hospital and the day after we'd signed the hospice papers, when Bob complained of pain, he got his first and only ministration from hospice: a minimum-dose morphine pill. I questioned the need, saying that Darvon had always worked, but the hospice nurse assured me the morphine would be better and make him "more comfortable." I kissed Bob and told him to sleep well.

"I sure do love you," he said, and smiled.

That night, or more precisely at 1:15 in the early morning of Sunday, November 6, exactly two months and five days after our escape from flooded Memorial Hospital, a tiny, dark-haired nurse shook me as I slept in the fold-out chair next to Bob's bed. "He's gone," she said.

I shot upright. "What? What do you mean?"

"He's gone," she repeated. Although she had come into the room earlier and found Bob in distress, his breathing irregular and his heartbeat erratic, she didn't wake me until too late.

I rushed to Bob's bed. His eyes were open, his skin already feeling chilled, his mouth frozen in an expression of astonishment. I don't know the immediate cause of death. An embolism might have killed him, or maybe he reacted to the morphine. Nobody mentioned an autopsy, and though now I wish I'd insisted, just so I'd know, I suppose an autopsy would have been superfluous. The obituary later said Bob died "peacefully." I'm not sure that was true, even though I was in the room with him. Perhaps his death was peaceful. I'd like to believe that like the patient Gloucester in *King Lear*, his heart "burst smilingly."

Bob met the stone wall alone.

The death certificate listed cancer as cause of death. It should also have listed Katrina, the United States Army Corps of Engineers, and the Department of Homeland Security.

News coverage in the early weeks of October had continued to focus on the stricken Gulf Coast, and especially New Orleans. Bob and I had watched from our rented apartment in Dallas as the water slowly drained from the neighborhoods of New Orleans and surrounding suburbs. In the weeks that followed, the death count rose steadily. Victims were found in many areas, from the affluent neighborhoods of Lakeview and parts of New Orleans East to the poorer regions of the Lower Ninth Ward. The dead lay inside the wreckage of attics and in rooms where sodden walls now sprouted spores of mold. Corpses were found outside in the open trapped in trees, under bushes, or beneath the rusting remains of cars, trucks, and boats. Victims were recovered from all of the city's flooded hospitals, including the hallways and chapel at Memorial, and from nursing homes that failed to evacuate their elderly residents. Relatives searched for missing loved ones, and many were forced to search long-distance, from cities all over the country where evacuees had found shelter. A makeshift morgue took shape in St. Gabriel, Louisiana, a small town seventy-five miles upriver from New Orleans near Baton Rouge, where officials tried to tally and identify bodies delivered daily.

Meanwhile, engineers came to New Orleans from other parts of the country and from abroad to study the broken levees. One thing soon became clear: the deluge that swamped New Orleans was not a natural disaster. Hurricane Katrina was the catalyst, yes—but the flood was the fault of collapsed walls and weakened levees. The New Orleans flood protection system had been poorly designed, constructed "on the cheap" so that specifications were ignored and corners cut, and then overseen by a levee board of political appointees lacking expertise, whose oversight and maintenance consisted of meetings where attention was paid more to lunch than to levees. And once the Corps of Engineers' levees failed, the death, devastation, and suffering were exacerbated by the incredible ineptness of other government officials and agencies who delayed rescues, prevented access to needed supplies, and in so many ways failed in their mission to respond. Who can forget the photograph of hundreds of yellow school buses, sitting empty and unused in a city lot while thousands of stranded New Orleanians waited in blazing heat outside the Convention Center for transportation that didn't come? In every sense, the 2005 drowning of New Orleans was a man-made disaster.

My husband was one of its victims, though he's not included in any official tally.

Yes, Bob's cancer was aggressive and would have killed him eventually. But the horrific experience at Memorial surely hastened his death. How much longer might he have lived if his treatment hadn't been interrupted? If he hadn't had to endure the strain of sitting hour after hour in that broken wheelchair in 100°-plus temperatures, then sleeping on the filthy floor of a garage that had become a cesspool? If he hadn't been subjected to that harsh and jolting passage up the stairs to the roof, followed by the stress of being ferried in an open helicopter over the flooded city to an unknown destination? Bob arrived in Thibodaux with a bacterial infection and a collapsed lung. The daily shots of blood-thinning medication prescribed to keep another pulmonary embolism from forming had stopped while he was trapped at Memorial. Did that interruption allow another deadly clot to form?

The ordeal Bob suffered in flooded New Orleans robbed us of time.

Taking Bob's body back to be buried in New Orleans was not an option. The city's major funeral homes had been flooded and were still closed. Tombs in New Orleans are customarily above ground, since so much of the city sits below sea level, and cemeteries and mausoleums had been heavily damaged by the water that stood for weeks before finally draining away, leaving crypts disturbed and coffins displaced. Grounds were choked and yellowed by salt water. The city was struggling to cope with more than a thousand bodies already there, most being "processed" upriver in St. Gabriel, in the temporary morgue. New Orleans was not ready to deal with its living, let alone its dead.

So on November 9, we had the funeral in Dallas, on the cemetery grounds in a small free-standing chapel reminiscent of the dark grey stone of the English Lake District that we loved. The priest who had met Bob in the hospital and given him last rites conducted a simple service. We did manage to give it a New Orleans flavor. We bought recordings of "Just a Closer Walk With Thee" and "I'll Fly Away." Aaron Neville's rendition of "Ave Maria" played. Afterward, my brother and Bob's nephews and grandnephews carried the oaken casket out of the chapel and placed it in a glass-walled carriage drawn by two sleek black horses. My sisters found a red umbrella, and Liz trimmed it with beads and black fringe. I held it high as the small congregation walked behind the carriage in a New Orleans-style second line, led by a three-piece band whose drummer beat a slow cadence before bursting into "When the Saints Go Marching In."

I tried my best to dance.

Chapter Eleven

Shoring Up Ruins

Post-K

New Orleans was awash with grief in the months after the flood. I made a brief visit in late November. Two weeks had passed since Bob's funeral, and still I felt suspended, adrift, numb with disbelief. Returning to New Orleans and our house would be hard, but I needed to go back.

Landing at Armstrong International Airport, I looked out at nearly empty runways and vacant gates. Inside, the terminal seemed deserted, all the shops closed and dark, only a few workers at their posts and scattered passengers scuttling down long, silent hallways. The memory of the suffering hordes crowded in the sweltering heat of the terminal that day in early September quickened my steps, and I rushed to escape. I'd left our car in Dallas, so I boarded the van bound for the rental car lots.

As I drove from the airport through the suburbs and into New Orleans, the wounded city seemed abandoned, enveloped in silence and dust. Blue tarps flapped on roofs, covering holes where people had chopped their way out of attics to escape rising water. In the shadows under highway overpasses, along roadsides, or overturned in yards sat the hulking wrecks of hundreds of rusting vehicles, caked with mud and covered in grey dust, their windshields opaque. Block after block of damaged buildings lined the streets, brown lines tracing the mark of floodwater on their sides. The florescent orange or red X's painted by rescuers, noting dates of search and numbers of bodies or animals found, glowed strangely high up the sides of some of the houses. It took a moment to register that many of the marks had been made by people in boats, floating high above ground-floor windows.

Parked in front of our house, I sat for a long time before steeling myself to approach the gate. Last time I'd been here, that September day during the curfew, I'd left Bob in Thibodaux, alive, still believing he'd return to this house he loved.

I held my breath as I opened the door, but the blast of decay that had reached out to grab my sisters and me in late September had faded. What was left was a muted, musty, vaguely nose-wrinkling smell. The front rooms of the house were silent and dark, the shutters still closed against hurricane winds. In a corner of the living room, the sight of the soft leather chair where Bob spent so many hours—he called it "my excellent chair"—socked me in the gut. How could it be that I'd never again see him in that chair?

I bolted toward the back of the house, to the large space that was kitchen, sitting, and dining room. This was the heart of the house, the room we'd most loved. If I was going to be able to stay here, somehow this room would let me know. The light from the unshuttered transom windows cast a soft glow, reflected in the glass of the cypress cabinet in the corner. Under a film of dust, the dark granite of the counters glinted. A sob escaped from somewhere deep as I pictured Bob sitting at the round pine table, looking out at the greens of the courtyard and the old cypress fence he loved, a glass of pinot noir in his hand, smiling and happy. Home.

It seemed a million years ago that we had created this room. Like many renovations, ours had been full of unexpected problems. We both had a vision in our heads of what we wanted the back room to be: an interior extension of the courtyard, a calm haven. Yet as difficulties and costs multiplied, our stress levels rose. Finally Bob announced he'd had enough.

"We'll finish the job, and then we'll put the house on the market."

"Okay," I said, "but let's not cut corners. Let's do everything the way we'd want it if we were staying."

One morning weeks later, after all the mess, bill-paying, and conflicts with contractors were finally over, Bob looked around at the newly painted pale sage walls, the welcoming kitchen, the shiny green ginger leaves and red-tinted banana fronds waving in the brick courtyard outside glass doors and folded his arms contentedly.

"I love this room," said Bob. "I love this house." He never spoke of selling it again.

Now I shook my head. We thought that renovation was stressful. We hadn't known what stress was. I gazed at the silent emptiness and took a long breath.

My brother Bill arrived within the hour, armed with industrial-strength deodorizers and ready for clean-up duty.

"It's hard to know where to start," I told him.

"Let's start in the kitchen. I'm good at kitchens."

So we donned rubber gloves and got to work. The hundreds of black flies that had clustered on walls and cabinets around the stinking refrigerator back in September were gone. Now a gaping emptiness was left where the fridge had been. The thin copper pipe that had been attached to the ice maker was bent back, jutting into space. The fridge still sat beyond the French doors, pitched on its side in the overgrown courtyard beneath tattered banana leaves. Inside, covering the pale walls and white cabinets were thick clumps of raised black specks, hundreds of them, droppings left behind by the flies. The pine floor in the kitchen felt sticky from the residue of the maggots, and dust dulled the old heart pine boards throughout the house. Bill and I spent two days scraping, cleaning, and polishing every surface, glad to have a task that at least seemed do-able. A man from Entergy appeared miraculously on the promised day to turn on the gas, a small sign of progress.

On the third day, Bill returned to Raleigh and I flew back to Dallas, back to the rented apartment and a Thanksgiving without Bob. Before heading for the airport, we detoured through sections of the Ninth Ward and Lakeview, stunned at the utter silence, the wrecks of houses on block after desolate block. TV and photographs didn't convey the immense scope of the destruction. My

God, I thought. How can this ever be fixed? And we were seeing only a small fraction of the eighty percent of the city that had flooded.

The airport terminal was once more eerily empty. Footsteps echoed. Again my imagination peopled the spaces in the cavernous lobby with crowds of ghostly wheelchairs and stretchers. Hanging high in the air was the flying figure of Icarus.

Five weeks later, just as New Orleans prepared to usher in the New Year, I moved back for good.

"Are you sure you want to go back?" my sister Liz had asked. "So much is ruined. It's not going to be an easy place to live right now."

"No place will be easy without Bob," I said. "At least I have a house to go back to, unlike so many. I guess that makes me lucky." I sighed. "I'm not sure, but going back feels right."

"Rebuilding the city is going to take work," said Rainy. "Maybe eventually you'll find ways to get involved."

So my sisters helped me clear out the Dallas apartment, and in late December we drove together down the spine of Louisiana, past small towns and along stretches of soy and cane fields, still looking battered from Hurricane Rita's passage. Finally we rolled over the Crescent City Connection, spanning the Mississippi River, into downtown New Orleans.

Four months after the flood, New Orleans felt like a cross between a frontier outpost and the remains of a war zone. Streets were littered with huge piles of debris and lined with carcasses of rusted, dust-caked cars, trucks, and boats. Small signs on wooden stakes bloomed in the neutral grounds of streets and avenues: "Roof Repairs Cheap," "Will Gut Houses," "Mold Abatement." Rows of empty, rusting refrigerators lined sidewalks on every block, their doors sometimes wrapped with silver duct tape or decorated with spray-painted messages to Katrina, FEMA, the Corps of Engineers, or other villains. Walking the sidewalks of the French Quarter, we encountered people still looking shell-shocked, their eyes pinched and distant. Jeep loads of armed National Guardsmen patrolled the streets. Stores and restaurants were gradually re-opening, but many were still closed and some were gone for good. A grey dust covered everything, and a fetid odor permeated the air, a mixture of rot and burgeoning mold.

The grocery on our corner was open again for limited hours, and John Matassa was back at his usual spot in front of the door, surveying the neighborhood and greeting familiar customers. His brother Louis stood just inside.

"Hey," John said when I walked up. "Are y'all back? How's Bob?"

I thought I was prepared, but tears I couldn't hold back erupted when I told the Matassas that Bob had died.

Their faces showed momentary shock, then concern. "I'm sorry," Louis said, his tone somber. Then, after I'd given them the basic details, he said, "How're you doing?"

"You let us know if you need anything," John added. Their eyes expressed a sad weariness, as if this was one more among many stories they'd heard in the past weeks, too many stories of suffering and loss.

Inside, the crowded store seemed the same, but the smell was different. Overlaying the pungent scents of red beans and gumbo from the deli was a vague new odor. The freezers and refrigerated cases had been cleaned, but the store had a funky smell that would linger for weeks, a mixture of cleaning fluids and the remnants of rot and mold. Yet customers in the aisles were cheerful, glad to have this valued neighborhood fixture open again.

Paula from around the corner greeted me at the produce case, immediately inquiring about Bob. I would have to get used to telling people he was gone. After giving her a brief version of our story, I asked how she and her husband had fared.

"We stayed at home," she said. "The day of the storm wasn't bad—just long, with no power and that wind that never stopped. Next day was worse. No flooding here, but we listened to the radio, and the looters had us really scared. We could hear yelling and gun shots in the street. Everything was so dark. That was a bad night. Wednesday we packed up and left. We had Trident with us, and we figured the huge dog in the car would keep us from being stopped or carjacked. We made it to Baton Rouge. Came back last month. Now we're fighting the insurance company to get our roof fixed."

She wasn't alone. In the coming weeks, we would all learn about the bewildering maze of red tape and bureaucracy people all over the city had to contend with before they could start repairing their homes and putting their lives back together. The day before, the front page of the *Times-Picayune* had blared a typical note of frustration: "FEMA Guidelines Baffle Public." Now as I left Matassa's, I glanced at the rack by the door, holding papers with similar headlines: "Wait Times for Adjustors Drag On" and "The Check's Not in the Mail."

Loan and grant programs kept promising that victims would be "made whole." Hearing about people who lost their homes and all their possessions made me sad, yet I sometimes found myself grimly wishing I could trade places.

The traditional New Year's Eve fireworks display was scheduled as usual, but late on the afternoon of the 31st, a heavy fog crawled in from the Mississippi, blanketing the French Quarter. Like so much in post-Katrina New Orleans, the fireworks had to be canceled. But the city announced that New Year's Eve music in Jackson Square would go on. The start of 2006 would be marked not by the usual maniacal-looking baby dropping at midnight onto the roof of Jax Brewery but this time by a giant, flamboyantly-colored gumbo pot.

A little after 10:00 p.m., my sisters Rainy and Liz and I set out walking toward Jackson Square. The old street lights cast a ghostly glow in the thick fog, and colored Christmas lights on some of the wrought iron balconies glimmered. The crowd gathered around the Square was smaller than in previous years. An odd mix of people—all races, all ages—milled in the barricaded streets: contract workers and volunteers brought to the city by FEMA or other agencies, Spanish-speaking itinerant laborers new to New Orleans, many locals who had returned from exile, and a core group of die-hard residents who had never left. Some revelers carried plastic flutes of champagne or go-cups of beer and wore the usual hats, feather boas, or neon spectacles flashing "2006," but the overall mood was subdued, a kind of muted celebration, as if people were glad to greet a new year with familiar rituals but still weighed down by the loss and devastation we all were living with. Earlier in the day, a jazz funeral procession in memory of flood victims had wound through Uptown streets, and a candlelight ceremony was planned for midnight in the Ninth Ward. Now Jackson Square seemed a small oasis of light in the grey fog. High on the roof at the edge of the Square, overlooking the river, the red neon *JAX* sign glowed in the mist.

The Coolbone Brass Band played on a stage near the entrance to the Square, facing the river. The pale spires of St. Louis Cathedral lit up the background. The crowd drew close, people in pairs and in groups, swaying to the music in the damp, foggy air. The tangy smell of boiling crawfish wafted from a corner café, mixed with the scent of chicory and the sharp, watery smell of the Mississippi. I thought of Bob, and the many New Year's Eves we'd stood right here, arms entwined, celebrating the start of another year.

When Arlo Guthrie took the stage, a wave of emotion pulsed through the crowd. Arlo had organized a train trip on the famous *City of New Orleans*, riding the rails from Chicago to New Orleans to raise funds for musicians affected by Katrina and the flood. Along the route, assorted fellow musicians had boarded the train and they'd played benefit concerts at stops along the way. The crowd in Jackson Square listened intently as Arlo talked about the trip and the money that would buy new instruments for the city's musicians and school bands, and they cheered when he declared that New Orleans would rise again.

The opening strains of the classic song "The City of New Orleans" brought a louder cheer, but as the verses began, the crowd got suddenly quiet, as if everyone was listening intently to the often-heard words that now resonated with new meaning:

Passin' graves that have no name,
Freight yards full of old black men
And the graveyards of rusted automobiles.

Then the familiar chorus rang out—*Good mornin' America,*
how are you?/ Don't you know me, I'm your native son—
and hundreds of voices joined in, getting louder until all of
Jackson Square rang with the defiant refrain: *I'm the train*
they call the City of New Orleans/ I'll be gone five hundred
miles when the day is done.

I sang at the top of my voice, thinking of Bob,
thinking of the city. All around, people swayed with the
music, arms locked and voices raised, faces wet with tears.

Rainy and Liz flew home a few days later, and for the first
time, I was on my own in New Orleans, truly alone. They
say grief is different for each individual. The grief I felt
seemed to fit all the clichés. It hit me in waves,
unexpectedly. A sudden memory of Bob, or a simple
question from a concerned friend—"How are you?"—could
trigger helpless weeping.

I tried to busy myself with all the paperwork
necessitated by death. I met with the insurance adjustor,
who came to assess the damage to roof, walls, and ceilings.
I was lucky to know a talented contractor who had worked
on the house in the past. He was back, and he arranged for
the minor repairs the 165-year-old house needed: replacing
slates that had blown off the roof, re-glazing a broken
window pane, repairing interior cracks and leaks in walls
and ceilings. On appointed days, the house swarmed with
Mexican and Central American painters, plasterers or
roofers. Meanwhile, I tried to focus on day-to-day tasks. I
made frequent trips to Matassa's grocery and down the
block to the Postal Emporium. I reconnected with French
Quarter friends, and I chatted on sidewalks or in store
aisles with neighbors or new acquaintances. "Are you
back?" and "How'd you make out?" were the ritual
questions all over the city. Self-pity was impossible:
everybody had a Katrina story of danger or hardship or
loss.

As news of Bob's death spread among friends and former colleagues in Pennsylvania, condolence messages came in sporadically. Most touching were those from former students. Ron, an athlete who'd been Bob's student and advisee and the first of his family to graduate from college, told me "If it wasn't for Professor Perry, I'd never have stayed in school. I loved and respected him, and you two were like family. I'm trying to teach my 8-year-old son the way Professor Perry taught me." Jeffrey, an English major who had left Pennsylvania to study abroad, wrote that he'd finished his Master's thesis and listed on its dedication page: "Robert Perry, who gave me magic and Shakespeare in return for grief at Hector's death." Jeff recalled visiting Bob's office to discuss the *Iliad* and telling Bob he had enrolled in the next semester's Shakespeare class. He was stunned when Bob pulled a massive *Complete Works of Shakespeare* from his shelf and gave it to him, then and there. For Jeff, Bob became teacher, mentor, friend. Donna, who years ago worked for me as a tutor in a program for high-risk students, wrote to say she recalled Bob and me so often walking together on campus, clearly loving each other and our work. After years in a happy marriage herself, she realized now that Bob and I had been important role models. There were others, and thinking of all the lives Bob influenced was a comfort. But it didn't stop the pain.

Memories ambushed me. Walking down Dumaine Street, I looked at the empty façade of what had been the Quarter Scene restaurant, said to have been a favorite haunt of Tennessee Williams, and saw myself sitting with Bob at that table in the front window, lingering over coffee and laughing while we waited for a lashing rain to let up. A new restaurant eventually opened in that space, but the Quarter Scene, like Bob, was gone. Passing the empty windows of a specialty clothing store on Royal Street behind the cathedral, I saw Bob's face reflected in the glass. He loved that store's fanciful displays of exotic-looking mannequins posed insouciantly in glittering gowns and fabulous hats, their scenes adding glamor and whimsy to that alley bordering the cathedral garden. We would often detour just to see those window displays, now vanished. Sitting alone on a bench in Jackson Square brought a cascade of memories of Bob, praising the azaleas, commenting on the antics of the clowns and mimes on the corners, smiling at the sounds of the brass bands playing near the cathedral. I walked alone by the river and heard his voice, remarking on the churning currents or the water's height, humming along with the riverboat's calliope. Loss shadowed my days.

I wrestled with feelings of guilt. Could I have made his last months easier, happier, better? Was I wrong to urge him for so long to fight? What more might I have done to make sure he knew how special and loved and cherished he was?

The weeks passed, and most days I felt like a sleepwalker, going through empty motions. I had moments of the "magical thinking" Joan Didion wrote about after the death of her husband. I gave bags of clothes to charity, including some of Bob's shoes, but certain pieces of clothing stopped me. No, that shirt was his favorite—I can't give that away. Or, those comfortable shoes he always wore —I should keep those. I was told I had to close our joint bank account and became incensed. Why make me close that account? I delayed for months—Bob managed that account, he wouldn't want it closed. I renewed some of his memberships and kept his name on subscriptions. All my life a voracious reader, I now had trouble focusing on anything longer than a magazine article. I felt buffeted, disoriented, unmoored. The word *loneliness* doesn't begin to describe what suddenly was the total *not-there-ness* of the person I'd loved and lived with for thirty-six years.

The unbearable absence.

I had to contend with anger, too. Anger that Bob had to suffer being marooned at Memorial. Anger at the Dallas nurse who didn't wake me as he lay dying. Anger at all that positive thinking we'd been urged to do. Anger that my generous, good husband had his life cut short by a disease that years of research hadn't conquered, and anger at the precious time we spent on treatments that didn't work.

. . .

Anger filled the city as well, expressed on radio talk shows or in the daily newspaper. Day after day in calls or letters, citizens railed at government ineptitude and the slow pace of recovery, at the Corps of Engineers who weren't repairing the failed levees strongly enough or fast enough, at lack of leadership and direction, at housing agencies whose policies were keeping so many residents in exile, unable to return to their homes and their city.

"Coming home" was a phrase I heard over and over. As the months passed, it became clear that many New Orleanians who had been suddenly uprooted to parts of the country as close as Texas and as far away as California and New England were choosing to stay, to start over in new places. Some wanted to escape ever again facing the threat of hurricanes or floods. Some decided to put down roots with far-flung family who gave them shelter, and some found better opportunities elsewhere. Others said they couldn't stand to return to a devastated New Orleans that would never be "like it was."

My sisters had been right: the ruined city was not an easy place to live in that year after the deluge. Whole sections stayed dark, waiting for electricity to be restored. Sewer pipes leaked all over town, and water pressure in my kitchen would suddenly plummet without warning. Each time I drove on major streets like St. Charles Avenue, I found makeshift stop signs still at many intersections—traffic lights stayed dark, some bent and sprouting disconnected wires. Streetcars were sidelined by broken cables and washed-out tracks, and bus service was curtailed. Pot holes, always a bane that made driving in New Orleans an adventure, reached epic proportions. A chasm opened on a block of St. Louis Street in the Quarter and seemed to grow by the week—mules pulling buggies learned to maneuver around it. The French Quarter had not flooded and was relatively unscathed, yet the sidewalks Bob and I had strolled so happily, taking pleasure in the scent of jasmine and the purple bursts of bougainvillea, enjoying the carefree cheer of fellow residents and the enthusiasm of visitors, now fronted too many empty spaces. Restaurants and stores, some established decades ago, were gone. A fierce determination to hang on to the elements that had made the city unique gripped all of us survivors, and each re-opening of a familiar place was greeted with celebration. Still the fact remained: New Orleans had suffered a sea change.

Thousands of citizens yearned to come back and rebuild their lives in their old neighborhoods of the city they called home. I often drove past the Iberville and Lafitte projects near the French Quarter in the section of the city called Tremé. Sturdy brick buildings built on high ground in the early 1940s by Creole craftsmen, the Iberville was largely undamaged and although some of the Lafitte buildings had minor flooding, apartments on upper floors escaped. Residents had been allowed to return to some of the apartments, but most were boarded up tight, sitting empty and dark like other complexes in the city.

When the U. S. Department of Housing and the Housing Authority of New Orleans announced plans to demolish the low-income projects and build new developments—eventually—rather than renovate and allow families stuck in distant cities to reclaim their homes, anger flowed into the streets. Grass roots groups organized marches and displaced residents traveled to New Orleans to join in, some sleeping in tent villages surrounding the fenced-off complexes, proposing to do the clean-up themselves if they could just get in. Bill Quigley, the banner-carrying attorney who helped me in the Memorial garage, was among the early returnees to New Orleans, helping in the fight to re-open affordable housing.

I turned daily to the pages of obituaries in the paper. Bob and I had always been fascinated by the *Times-Picayune's* obituaries, with thumbnail pictures above names such as "Simoneaux" and "Bourgeois," often including colorful nicknames ("Sausage Nose," "Tum Tum," a mail carrier called "Turtle") of people who hadn't simply died but "slipped into eternity," or been "called home." Now, with a far smaller population, the obituary pages were longer than ever. Well into the first half of 2006, entries appeared listing date of death as August 29, 30, or 31, 2005, signifying that another victim of the flood had been identified. Every day, the pages listed people who had died in distant places—Texas, Georgia, Mississippi, other cities in Louisiana or in states all over the country. They were described as "life-long residents of New Orleans until Katrina," or "Katrina refugee," and I wondered how many of their deaths could be blamed, like my husband's, partly on the physical hardship and stress of evacuation. The exiled dead included many older faces, people for whom the ordeal of being uprooted, of losing relatives, homes, or possessions must have been especially traumatic. How many, like Bob, died prematurely?

Younger faces were pictured, too. Uncertainties about money, missing family, disrupted medical care, or the stress of rebuilding surely affected the health of people of all ages who had watched their lives wash away. It was said that suicides had increased but were sometimes being acknowledged only as "accidental" deaths. Mental health services were almost nonexistent. Crime in New Orleans seemed to burgeon like mold, and the faces of murdered young people stared out from the obituary pages, victims of predators returning from exile or new to the city, taking advantage of a weakened police force and a barely functional justice system. Long after the floodwaters receded, the people of New Orleans were still suffering fallout from the disaster.

Bob was one of the uncounted. Who knows when the final toll of victims of Katrina will be tallied?

The Memorial Medical Center complex where Bob and I were trapped stayed closed, fenced off, dark and abandoned. Small notices finally appeared in the newspaper, announcing that doctors and patients could retrieve their files, and I pictured rooms full of moldering manila folders and soggy papers. I considered trying to get Bob's records to add to the collection I'd kept, but the thought of re-entering that hospital stopped me.

Seeing my tote bag full of Bob's medical records resting in a corner of the bedroom stopped me, too. Why keep them? I told myself there was no reason, yet I stuffed them in the back of a cabinet. The notebooks full of written reports, the computer images that came from scans and tests, the set of dark, old-fashioned x-rays showing cloudy outlines of internal organs—somehow they seemed a physical connection I couldn't bring myself to break.

One morning, a headline in the *Times-Picayune* drew my eye: Tenet Healthcare was selling the complex known as Memorial to Ochsner Health System, a not-for-profit system with a nearby hospital and clinics throughout the New Orleans area. Ochsner said part of the complex would soon re-open and decreed that henceforth the facility would be known as "Ochsner Baptist." So the old name locals had always used was back, and "Memorial," with all its connotations of disaster, was relegated to history.

I wondered whether any of the former staff would return to the new Baptist. Would Nurse Carolyn or any of the other nurses go back to that place where they and their patients were marooned? What had happened to those people who worked so desperately to get all of us out?

One unexpected answer came not long after Ochsner publicized its plans. Louisiana Attorney General Charles Foti called a press conference to announce the arrests of a respected physician, Dr. Anna Pou, and two nurses, accusing them of killing four patients at Memorial Hospital in the days after the storm by administering a "lethal cocktail," a combination of morphine and the sedative Versed, with the intent of causing death. The deceased were patients in a separate critical care facility, LifeCare, housed on the seventh floor of the flooded Memorial complex. Traces of both drugs had been found in the bodies of the four patients, and the Attorney General said Dr. Pou and the two nurses had been seen carrying syringes in the hallway outside the alleged victims' rooms.

Rumors of what the press sometimes called "mercy killings" and other times "euthanasia" at Memorial had surfaced soon after the flood. In October, 2005, while we waited in the Dallas apartment, I had read in the *Dallas Morning News* that the Attorney General had begun issuing subpoenas and talking with witnesses who were trapped at the flooded hospital. Yet the arrests of the three women nine months later shocked the city of New Orleans. Attorney General Foti accused the women of playing God and said they were guilty not of euthanasia but of "plain and simple homicide."

Every article written about the case brought back memories of those frightening days Bob and I were trapped with two thousand others in the fetid heat of that flooded hospital. The doctors and nurses I encountered had worked day and night to comfort and care for patients in the dangerous conditions before help finally came. The accusations against these three were hard to believe, and their harsh treatment by the Attorney General seemed particularly cruel. All three women were arrested unexpectedly in their homes, at night—the doctor was still wearing scrubs after surgery—and dramatically accused in a press conference that seemed orchestrated for maximum publicity. Like many in the city, I wondered at the motives and the methods.

Dr. Pou and the nurses vehemently denied any guilt. Fellow doctors and nurses leapt to their defense, pointing out that the accused were among those who voluntarily stayed behind to care for patients in the horrific conditions of the flooded hospital. Medical experts claimed that far from being a "lethal cocktail," the drugs found in the deceased were commonly prescribed to relieve pain and suffering for critically ill patients. Yet the families of the deceased claimed their relatives would have lived were it not for the actions of Dr. Pou and the nurses. Other medical staff on duty during those desperate days at Memorial insisted the plan was to evacuate every patient and discounted the possibility that this doctor, a cancer specialist who had a reputation for excellence and dedication to her patients, would deliberately cause any patient's death.

The case made its way slowly through the system, finally being sent to a Grand Jury, even though six months after the arrests, the Orleans Parish Coroner officially classified the four deaths as "undetermined" and told the *Times-Picayune* "the evidence collected does not support a finding of homicide." The Grand Jury deliberated for months, finally compelling the two nurses to testify by granting them immunity. Public support grew for Dr. Pou. Hundreds of people gathered at a rally in City Park, and opinions in letters, blogs, and call-in shows came down heavily on her side. Finally, in late July, fully a year after the three women had been arrested, their lives and careers interrupted, the Grand Jury refused to indict Dr. Pou, and the Orleans Parish District Attorney dropped all charges against her and the nurses. The doctor, who all along professed total innocence of anything but trying to make patients at the flooded hospital "comfortable," still faced civil law suits brought by the patients' families and continued accusations from the Attorney General's office. Mr. Foti said of the Grand Jury, "I regret their decision," and maintained that the district attorney's office failed to call relevant witnesses. Voters responded by defeating Attorney General Foti's bid for re-election.

I don't know whether I encountered that particular doctor or those nurses during our nightmarish time in the flooded Magnolia garage. I do know the physicians, nurses, other staff, and volunteers I saw during those dreadful days worked tirelessly and selflessly to care for the patients in their charge and to get all of us out. At least one nurse was injured trying to load a patient onto a helicopter, and some have reported lasting effects, both mental and physical, from the ordeal. The hospital's owner was unprepared for disaster and although Tenet finally organized a rescue, staff at Memorial functioned without help for days, forced to improvise in desperate conditions. Except for the Coast Guard and to some extent the National Guard, government agencies were useless at best. Without the dedicated efforts of Memorial's staff, the death toll at that hospital would surely have been far higher.

As repeated anniversaries of the flood approached, no charges had been brought against any of the engineers, contractors, levee overseers, or government officials whose actions or negligence caused over a thousand deaths and terrible destruction in New Orleans.

Nor had any of them been arrested, much less at night, in their homes.

I tried for over a year to find Nurse Carolyn Bowers. The phone number she'd given me had been disconnected, and I couldn't find another. I wondered whether she was one of the many nurses who left New Orleans and found jobs in other places. I searched for her on the internet with no luck. Then I thought of contacting Dr. Richard Deichmann, whose book *Code Blue: A Katrina Physician's Memoir,* chronicling his experience as Chief of Medicine at Memorial/Baptist during the disaster, had appeared the previous year. He suggested I call the nursing administration office at Ochsner, and not long before the second anniversary of Katrina, I made that call.

"Carolyn Bowers?" said the voice that answered. "She's up on Five, I'll transfer your call."

So I finally found her, working as a hematology/ oncology nurse at Ochsner Hospital in adjacent Jefferson Parish. When she answered the phone, I told her my name. "You were my husband's nurse at Baptist during the flood, and I've been trying to find you to thank you."

"Oh, my Lord," she said. "Are you the woman with the file box?"

She was amazed when I told her I'd gotten all my papers back. We met for lunch the following week, and Carolyn told me her story.

In the dark hours of Wednesday night, while caring for all of us trapped in Magnolia garage, Nurse Carolyn returned alone to the third floor of the hospital, hoping—in vain—to find a toilet that was still working.

"I knew there was a small staff bathroom at the back of the floor, and I thought maybe it would be useable. But it'd been found, and it wasn't. Overflowing like the rest of them." She made a face. "I was on my way back to the garage when I heard loud voices. I heard glass breaking and realized marauders were smashing the vending machines, so I hid in a closet 'til they were gone. Then I hightailed it back to the garage."

Once she got back to the garage, Carolyn and three other nurses decided to band together and stay in a group for the rest of their time in the flooded garage. All night, the four of them tended to patients lying on the garage floor. Then they helped to load the patients onto helicopters the next morning.

"There were some people in really bad shape in that garage," she said. "I was worried especially about a couple of patients from our floor who had bone marrow transplants just before the storm hit. They were really sick, and their immune systems were totally down. We tried to keep masks on them, in that awful heat. But we got them out."

"When did you get out?"

"Late Thursday afternoon, after all our patients were gone. I tried to get on a helicopter, but one of the nurses in our group freaked out—she didn't want to leave her dog, and she just had a total meltdown. By the time we got her calmed down, the helicopter had left. So I got out in a boat."

The boat took Carolyn and other staff out of the flooded garage and down Napoleon Avenue to the water's edge at St. Charles Avenue. There they transferred to an army truck that dropped them near the Lake Pontchartrain Causeway and the I-10 overpass, where—after working for six days straight—they joined a crowd of ten thousand people waiting for buses in the brutal heat. Tall LaShandra from the Oncology Unit and other colleagues were among that crowd, and the nurses huddled together amid the horde.

"There was no food," Carolyn said. "No water. Thousands of people and nobody in charge, only a few cops standing on the edges of the crowd. Then after awhile it started raining, hard. Rain poured down, and the ground turned swampy. No buses came, and no help. It was bad. The worst part was the bugs."

"Bugs?" In all I'd heard and read about conditions after the levees broke, nobody had mentioned bugs.

At nightfall that Thursday, clouds of mosquitoes flew in, tormenting the people waiting on the swampy ground, drawn by the lights on media trucks filming the miserable, helpless, increasingly angry crowd. "The mosquitoes were terrible," Carolyn said. "I had bites all over my body, we all did—you couldn't escape. People were getting agitated. It got dark. That night I was really afraid."

The group of nurses stayed together, and finally, near midnight, one of them spotted a relative. He worked for a local TV station, and he got them out, helping them to stow away on a media truck that took them to Baton Rouge and refuge with friends.

Only days into her evacuation, Carolyn learned that the Uptown house where she rented an apartment had caught fire and burned down. But within months she returned to New Orleans and easily found a job in a city desperate for nurses. About her experience at Memorial, Carolyn said, "I've put it all behind me. Haven't talked about it much."

Her silence wasn't unusual. When Bob and I had left Thibodaux a month after the disaster, arriving as refugees in Dallas, the young man who delivered Bob's new wheelchair to our apartment spoke with a recognizable accent. I told him we'd come from New Orleans, and his dark face brightened into a huge smile.

"Hey," he said. "I'm from New Orleans, too. Glad you made it out. God bless you."

We introduced ourselves and clasped hands and arms in a move that started as a handshake but became a hug, an instinctive greeting I later saw replicated among other survivors. His name was Darren. He called us "Miss Carolyn" and "Mister Bob." And like all New Orleanians who encountered each other in those days, he seemed eager to tell us his story. Darren and his wife and four-year-old son had been rescued after a day, a night, and another day on the roof of their Ninth Ward house. A boat had taken them to the Superdome, where they were separated.

"I got bused to Dallas. My wife ended up in Houston. She had my son with her, but in the shelter they got pulled apart somehow. My son stayed alone for three days before she found him."

"No," I said. "Three days—is he okay?"

"We think he gonna be all right. Didn't talk for awhile. Days and days he wouldn't say nothing, just stared out in space." Darren shook his head. "Got him in a school in Houston now. Seem to be doing okay. Still won't talk about the water, though."

The floodwaters had not reached the "little red schoolhouse," an elementary school in our French Quarter neighborhood, but the building had suffered some wind damage and stayed closed. Public schools all over New Orleans were abandoned by city officials, their doors and windows open to vandals and looters, roofs leaking and walls covered with mold. Private schools and universities rushed to reopen, but only a handful of city elementary and secondary schools were ready to accept students in the spring after the flood, and those were overcrowded, understaffed, and scrambled for textbooks and supplies. In the wake of the city's inertia, educators from the state and the private sector moved in, seizing the opportunity to transform a school system that even before Katrina had been among the nation's worst. Neighborhood schools gradually reopened, many as charter schools, and innovative young teachers from programs such as Teach for America came to the city, ready to create change.

That little red elementary school near our house reopened finally as an arts-centered charter school. Bob and I had always liked hearing the chattering voices of little ones parading up our street on their way to school, and it was nice to have them back, now wearing their purple, gold, or green uniform shirts emblazoned with the school's motto: "Work Hard. Be Nice." After a call for volunteer tutors in an elementary reading program caught my eye in late spring, I decided to get involved in upcoming years helping children learn to read.

Meanwhile, the slow recovery dragged on. President Bush had stood in Jackson Square less than two weeks after the federally-built levees failed and promised, "We will do what it takes" to bring New Orleans back, but the ineptitude the government showed during the disaster didn't just continue—it got worse.

Repairs to the city's infrastructure stalled while officials wrangled over reimbursement limits and labyrinthine rules from FEMA. Residents trickled back and white, boxy trailers appeared in driveways of ruined houses, though fields of trailers sat empty in neighboring states while applicants in New Orleans waited weeks and months for promised trailers that didn't come. Later, we would learn that many of the trailers that did arrive were contaminated by formaldehyde, and some people who lived in them for an extended time became ill from exposure. Thousands of residents and small business owners who wanted to come back needed funds from insurance, grant, or loan programs to repair their property but were left suspended, their decisions about rebuilding postponed by frustrating red tape and conflicting information. Urban planners and outside "experts" held endless meetings that produced few tangible results, and out-of-state corporations were given contracts to manage relief programs, collecting huge fees while causing waves of frustration and disappointment for applicants. Rents skyrocketed.

Of the millions of dollars in aid promised by the federal government or donated by concerned people worldwide, very little got swiftly to the people who desperately needed it. City officials blamed the state, state officials blamed Washington, and federal bureaucrats turned the blame back onto the city and state. New Orleans was adrift, with floundering leadership and no direction but a slowly-increasing populace determined to stay afloat. Unlike those indifferent sailors on Auden's ship who turned their backs on the drowning Icarus, former and new residents of New Orleans refused to sail away from disaster. Individual, volunteer, church, and neighborhood efforts became the forces driving recovery.

City churches slowly rebuilt their congregations, and Sunday scenes of joyous homecoming cheered spirits. People were still burdened—one Sunday at Our Lady of Guadalupe Church at the edge of the French Quarter, Cynthia, the choir director, sang a haunting, hymn-like rendition of "Nobody Knows the Trouble I've Seen" that brought tears to many eyes, and the diverse congregation often ended services by joining hands and singing "We Shall Overcome," an anthem that took on new meaning after Katrina. Yet people were determined to save the city, and every week, I encountered clusters of volunteers on French Quarter streets, sometimes wearing colorful tee shirts identifying them as members of some group or other, exploring the city on breaks from their work with organizations such as Habitat for Humanity and other non-profit and church-based groups. Volunteers of all ages, but especially college students who came on breaks, poured into New Orleans, sometimes from faraway places, to join local volunteers in rebuilding the city. Without them, recovery may have stalled indefinitely. As anniversaries of the disaster came and went, the flow of volunteers showed no signs of ebbing.

"Volunteer Bob" would have been glad to see the Audubon Aquarium of the Americas re-open nine months after the flood. A core group of staff and volunteers had worked faithfully to repair the building and keep its inhabitants alive. Aquariums and zoos in other cities had given shelter to surviving animals and offered replacements for those that were lost. An efficient web site was quickly designed to bring in donations, and money came from people all over the country and the world to help the aquarium, zoo, and other facilities recover. Restoring the aquarium's lost collection of fish will take years, but the beloved sea otters Buck and Emma were back, as was the giant sea turtle named Mydas.

From their comfortable exile in California, the New Orleans penguins were flown home in style, in a chartered plane provided by FedEx. I pictured a smiling Bob among the applauding onlookers as the nineteen penguins walked a red carpet to join the aquarium's other survivors, marching into the front door like celebrities.

In February, thoughts of New Orleanians habitually turned to Mardi Gras, the city's signature festival. Bob and I had been planning to don costumes on Mardi Gras for the first time the previous year, when his cancer was in remission. Chuckling, he announced he'd always wanted to mask in the Renaissance robes of the conniving Cardinal Wolsey. "I'll make a super Wolsey," he said, and I agreed, laughing at the thought of his newly-grown-in "chemo curls" under a cardinal's scarlet skull cap. I bought yards of red velvet and fake ermine trim for his costume and started to plan a nun's outfit for me. But Bob had spent that last Mardi Gras in a bed at Memorial Hospital, battling an infection while we listened to the sounds of brass bands marching down Napoleon Avenue in the Uptown parades. This year, the rolls of red velvet on the closet shelf seemed to come from another life.

Some people—mainly from outside New Orleans—expected officials to cancel Mardi Gras in 2006. The destruction was too great, they said, and the mood too dark for a party. Yet the mayor finally announced, after much indecision, that Mardi Gras would go on. Later it was said that the Zulu Social Aid and Pleasure Club, which was formed in 1909 by Creole and black laborers to spoof the all-white parades of traditional Carnival "royalty" and which had evolved into the city's premier organization for primarily African-American members, was instrumental in the decision to keep Mardi Gras alive. Timing was adjusted and some routes changed to fit the constraints of a reduced force of police and city workers, but the parades would roll. Most residents I talked to were not surprised.

"They can't cancel Mardi Gras," said David, behind the desk at the Postal Emporium. "If the city said no Mardi Gras, the people would make it happen."

A defiant mood took hold. Throughout the week before Fat Tuesday, parades rolled day and night. The disgust and frustration people felt at the bungling of officials on all levels found release in the native sense of humor and irony. Elaborate floats featured comical paper-maché figures of George W. Bush and FEMA's Michael Brown, with variations on the infamous line, "Brownie, you're doin' a heckuva job." The governor, the mayor, officials at FEMA, the Corps of Engineers, the Department of Homeland Security, insurance companies—all were lampooned in myriad creative ways. School bands, with improvised uniforms and borrowed instruments, strutted exuberantly behind the floats. Crowds lining the streets cheered loudly when the patched-together band called MAX appeared, made up of displaced students from St. Mary's, St. Augustine, and Xavier Prep, three schools whose legendary marching bands had been fixtures in past parades. Blue tarp festooned floats and was the costume fabric of choice.

The mood in the city was infectious. The merriment spilling onto the streets offered a respite from the grim tasks of clean-up, and from mourning. This would be a carnival tinged with sadness, for the city and for me, but I let myself be swept up in the spirit.

Bob and I had never experienced a New Orleans Mardi Gras in the days when we visited the city. To us the festival's reputation for drunken revelry and hordes of tourists was less than appealing, and even after we bought our house in the French Quarter, our teaching schedules usually kept us in Pennsylvania during those winter weeks leading up to Fat Tuesday. But in the spring of 1998, we spent an extended leave in New Orleans. We rented a small apartment Uptown and lived there while our house was being gutted. During those tense renovation weeks, our apartment was just a block off St. Charles Avenue, and that year we learned what Mardi Gras was all about.

The first parade was scheduled to roll down St. Charles on the evening of Friday the 13th and Bob had plastic go-cups ready. We carried our cups of wine out to the neutral ground, where sparse crowds were already gathered, waiting for the first sounds of the bands heralding the arrival of the Krewe of Oshun, named for an African goddess.

"Here it comes!" said Bob, as we prepared to watch quietly from the sidelines, sipping wine. Instead, we suddenly found ourselves ducking and dodging as strand after strand of glittering plastic beads pelted us, hurled by smiling masked riders shouting from elaborate floats. Being tall, Bob was a target and quickly perfected a one-armed catch, and I managed to grab some, too. Both our necks were soon chin-deep in multicolored beads as we kept trying for more, enjoying the high strutting of the high school bands and the enthusiasm of the riders amidst the laughter and screams of the milling crowds. We were hooked.

The next evening brought the Knights of Sparta, dressed in shining masks and medieval costumes, riding sleek horses down the center of St. Charles Avenue. Their parade was lit by traditional flambeaux, gas flames carried by dark-faced young men dressed in black, holdovers from century-old Mardi Gras history. For the next ten days, Bob and I were on the sidelines for every Uptown parade. Even in pouring rain, the parades rolled—we commiserated with and cheered the high school students in the bands marching down rain-drenched streets, covered in clear plastic but doggedly smiling, blowing their horns and strutting high behind drum majors who led them with whistles and kicks. We chatted with the friendly couples and families that lined the route and amassed bags and bags of purple, green, and gold beads, awed as the floats got bigger and more elaborate. Crowds especially loved the satiric floats, spoofing current events and parodying politicians. Laughter filled the air, and smiles flashed on every face.

Our excitement built as Fat Tuesday approached.

"Let's get up really early on Mardi Gras," said Bob. "I'll make Bloody Marys in time for Pete Fountain and the Half-Fast Marching Band." That group always rolled first, before the giant Zulu parade that traditionally preceded Rex, with its float carrying the King of Carnival.

"We'll have King Cake and Bloody Marys—a perfect New Orleans breakfast," I said.

We wandered out in plenty of time, but half of Uptown was already there. The sidewalks and St. Charles neutral ground were packed with families who had set up blankets, chairs and picnic paraphernalia. Children were perched high on wooden ladders topped with seats, giving them a vantage point for viewing and bead-catching. More than half of the spectators were in costume: there were clowns and fairy princesses, devils and angels, and imaginative family groups of pirates and chefs. Spirits were high.

"It's like a giant, magical street fair," I said. "I wish we had costumes."

But the costumes of the day soon appeared at the head of the Zulu parade. Two huge horses carried then-Mayor Marc Morial, dressed in black and masked as Zorro. Next to him rode Police Chief Richard Pennington, a Wild West gunslinger complete with lasso.

"Do you believe this city?" said Bob. "Where else could you see Pete Fountain leading Zorro the Mayor and a bunch of crazy royalty? Totally wacky. I love this place."

"Now that we have the house, it'll be fun to see what Mardi Gras is like in the French Quarter," I said. "I never realized it's a happy, city-wide party, but full of history, too. No wonder so many trees along St. Charles have beads hanging on them—now I see why."

New Orleans swept the streets on Ash Wednesday and got back to normal, and we returned to the work of renovation feeling a lot less stressed. The spirit of Mardi Gras had captured us both.

In February of 2006, my sister Lorraine was able to take time off work and flew in for her first experience of Mardi Gras in New Orleans, but now the crowds that lined the streets to watch parades seemed mostly home-grown, and the usual hordes of tourists were missing. Parade routes were lined with New Orleans families, some of them displaced residents who traveled back home from faraway places, re-uniting with friends and families for familiar celebrations in a transformed city. New amidst the throngs were the faces of itinerant Hispanic and Latino workers, who chattered in Spanish and stared in smiling amazement at the crazy masked riders hurling beads to the outstretched hands of the crowds. Many joined in with enthusiasm and caught their share of glittering green, purple, and gold strands.

On Fat Tuesday itself, the atmosphere pulsed with determined high spirits. The streets of the French Quarter teemed with topical costumes. Three women dressed as FEMA applications, covered head to toe in red tape. A group with aprons and chef hats set up a "Katrina Deli" on a block of Bourbon Street, offering a menu of Levee Leak Soup, Toxic Jambalaya, and Furniture Upside Down Cake, among other delicacies. There were blind levee inspectors with white canes, and insurance adjustors from hell, wearing devil costumes and horns. A family of five dressed as foil-covered Hershey kisses, a dig at Mayor Nagin's politically motivated description of New Orleans as "chocolate city." Rainy and I draped ourselves in white sheets and wore big, soft, bright yellow floppy hats and signs proclaiming us "Egg on the Face of FEMA." As we wandered the French Quarter, we got laughs and lots of comments. "Are ya fried or scrambled?" one man asked. We even got smiles from a few uncostumed people bravely wearing shirts or hats identifying them as FEMA workers.

Everybody was in a good mood, glad for a day to laugh in the face of troubles and celebrate living in a city that truly knows how to do both.

New Orleans' penchant for mixing laughter and tears certainly displayed itself in this first Mardi Gras post-Katrina. A shadow of melancholy passed over the merriment often. The Krewe of Muses parade featured a riderless float memorializing the victims who had perished in the storm and the flood, and in the back of everyone's mind was the knowledge that too many citizens were still in exile, unable to return for this celebration so central to the city's culture.

My sister and I found a spot on Canal Street for the Mid-city and Bacchus parades. Next to us was a large family of African-Americans, clearly native New Orleanians: they had their cooler of drinks and picnic baskets overflowing with fried chicken and other goodies, and they spoke in distinctive New Orleans cadences. The gray-haired grandmother held court in a folding chair, and two boys about eight ran back and forth, squeezing up to the barricades to catch handfuls of beads, then racing to bring them back to the piles stashed in bags by their grandmother's feet. They'd clearly had previous bead-catching experience.

Rainy asked one, "Are you in school here? Is school out for Mardi Gras?"

"Yes, ma'am," he answered. "We off the whole week. Not my cousin."

"You're not off for Mardi Gras?" I said to the other boy. "Where's your school?"

"Houston," he said. "Don't have Mardi Gras in Houston." He ran back for more beads.

We chatted with their mothers, standing nearby, and we learned that part of the family was home, but others were still staying in the places where they had evacuated, waiting for apartments they could move back to. The Houston contingent had made their first visit back to be here for Mardi Gras, but a brother and his family were still stuck in Arkansas, unable to get back even for a visit. "It's hard," one woman said, her eyes sad. "We all want to come home."

That word again: *home.* It seemed part of every conversation, all over the city. In the wake of destruction and displacement and loss, what did it mean to be "home"? For me, home had come to mean Bob: any place we were together was always home. Home was opening the door and hearing his voice calling out, "Is that you?" Home was a welcoming hug and quiet conversation at the end of the day. Home was shared struggles and shared laughter and a supportive, loving presence.

Where was home for me now? Was it Dallas, where we'd first met and fallen in love, and where Bob's body now lay alone, shaded by live oaks under the wide Texas sky? Was it Pennsylvania, where we'd been young and lived our middle years, through so many changes and so much history? Or was it New Orleans, whose siren song had drawn us, a city now struggling to rise from ruins but still stirring feelings of *home*?

I ended that post-K Mardi Gras by making my way with Rainy at dusk through the costumed throngs to an outside stage set up not far from the Mississippi River. There we heard Irma Thomas, New Orleans' Queen of Soul, do a show that set a perfect tone for that day of defiant celebration. Backed by a group of the city's best musicians, Irma sang upbeat classics that had people dancing in front of the stage or swaying in their portable chairs. But interspersed were slower songs, infused with the blues: "I'll Be Your Shelter in the Rain," and "Another Man Done Gone."

St. Charles Avenue on Sept. 26, 2005.

Canal Street on Sept. 26, 2005.

Funeral in Dallas, Nov. 9, 2005.

Second Line at the funeral, Nov. 9, 2005.

Epilogue

Music from a Farther Room

Thou'lt come no more;
Never, never, never, never, never.

Shakespeare, *King Lear* V.iii.305-6

Thirty-six years together, sixteen months of treatments, four days trapped in the floodwaters, and eight slow weeks of rehabilitation and decline—yet like Icarus slipping into the sea, Bob was with me and then, in an instant, he was not.

I'm coming to grips with my solitary life and the still strange status of *widow*. Not many people have tried to hand me that line about time healing, time easing the pain. No. Time spans a past of shared memories that now are mine alone. Ahead, time only extends the absence.

I re-read the letters Bob wrote to me during the five months before we married, when we were living in separate states. I kept all seventy of them. They bring alive his voice from long ago, and seeing his handwriting preserved on stationery his hands once held gives me a visceral sense of almost physical connection. His words evoke the confident, happy man, in witty control of his life, looking with love toward a future we'd share "for the long haul into place and time," writing that "the fates smiled knowingly when they wove the skeins of our lives together." He saved the letters I wrote to him, too, and reading those gives me a bittersweet glimpse of that long-ago young woman who predicted our love would deepen and endure over years that then seemed to stretch on forever.

Occasionally, I have found myself talking to him, sometimes in my head, but often out loud—and hearing my voice speaking to him doesn't seem odd, even now. It only reminds me that I'll never again hear him answer, or be startled into laughter at something he says, or benefit from his clear thinking or depth of knowledge or amazing memory. Or his encircling arms.

Bereft is the right word.

I still wake each morning to the painful moment: in his place beside me, Bob's not there.

In spring, the "walking" swamp iris Bob nurtured bloomed in our New Orleans courtyard, and the gardenia I planted when I returned after the storm produced its first sweet-scented flowers.

I made that trip back to England we'd talked about, traveling alone to some of the places that were special to Bob and me. On what would have been our thirty-eighth wedding anniversary, I saw a performance in London of *The Rose Tattoo,* the story of the grieving Serafina. Although it's not one of Tennessee Williams' most famous plays, this production was one I think both Bob and Tennessee would have liked. The play's Gulf Coast setting and comically poignant celebration of life and regeneration were powerful reminders of home.

Water followed me, too. In the weeks I was there, England was drenched with record rainfall and unusual flooding. When the Avon overflowed its banks in Stratford, flooding parks and streets and lapping toward theater steps, I snapped a photo and caught myself thinking, Wait 'til Bob sees this, he won't believe how high the water is. That night, in a theater near the swelling Avon, I saw Ian McKellen and the Royal Shakespeare Company bring to life *King Lear.* For the first time, I felt as well as understood that play, with its themes of aging and love and loss, its fruitless petitions to the gods, its "ripeness is all," and its haunting "never, never, never...."

Bob's absence was with me wherever I went, and often I felt as if I were inhabiting a scene where all color had been drained away, leaving everything painted in drab shades of black or grey. Yet as I sat alone at dinner in the Lake District one night, music played in the background. A guitar picked out a familiar melody, and with a shock I recognized it: *Just a little change, small to say the least....* Early the next morning, as I looked out over the misty lake, grey clouds shifted and a four-color rainbow, vivid and bright, arced over Windermere.

On my way home, I stopped in Pennsylvania. Each summer, for all the years we lived there, Bob looked forward to watching the lightning bugs glimmer in the yard behind our house. "Oh, wow," he'd say, calling me to the porch as darkness deepened. "Look—they're out there tonight." For a few years we'd missed them, and we feared that mosquito spraying had doomed the fireflies. This summer the fireflies were back, their tiny lights flickering above the shadowy grass.

At home in New Orleans, the plaintive fog horns moan on the river. Sometimes the faint melodies of the riverboat's calliope waft into the courtyard. Swamp iris pop up in new corners of the garden. On any random day, a brass band might round the corner and march down my street.

Acknowledgments

My abiding gratitude goes to the many dedicated nurses, doctors, support staff, and volunteers who cared for and evacuated patients and their families trapped in flooded Memorial/Baptist Hospital—few if any of them got the recognition and honor they deserve. Thanks also to the ambulance and flight personnel, the U. S. Coast Guard, the Fish and Wildlife Services, and the many selfless individuals who helped with rescues in New Orleans and all over the Gulf Coast after Katrina.

I'm grateful to the medical professionals who gave good care to my husband during his long months of treatment in New Orleans, Houston, Thibodaux and Dallas —a few I have named, but many I couldn't. They all have my gratitude.

Loving thanks to our family who searched for, helped, and cared for us: Nell, George, Beverley, Randy, Suzzi, Bill, Diane, and the other Perrys; my brother Bill, sister-in-law Samantha, and nephew Simon Flynn; and my sisters Lorraine Harrington and Elizabeth Fuchs. They are all part of our story and later helped me believe I could write it.

Special thanks to Carolyn Bowers, R.N., and LaShandra B. Sanders, R.N., who both talked to me about their time trapped at Memorial, and to Bill Quigley for his caring assistance in the hospital and subsequent encouragement.

This book took shape under the expert guidance of acclaimed writer James Nolan, to whom I'm enormously grateful. His creative writing workshops freed me from decades of academic prose and taught me how to tell a story, and his advice and insightful critiques made the story immeasurably better.

I thank the workshop members who read and responded to successive drafts, especially Marie-France Mourey, and also Jean Morgan Meaux, Celeste Berteau,

Joe Barbara, Nancy Barrett, Ed Bodker, Cheron Brylski, Genevieve Cancienne, Amy Conner, Don Downey, Rick Jervis, Deb Henkels, Adam Lair, Joe Landrum, Karen Laborde, Laura McNeal, Jacquelyn Milan, Ellie Rand, Maurice Carlos Ruffin, Aneela Shuja, Leslie Staub, Tricia Taylor, Melanee Usdin, and Susan Weaver.

Many friends and former colleagues encouraged me, and some read drafts of the manuscript, including Elaine Grove, Diana Lett, Virginia Martin, Richard Parker, Stan and Betty Wisniewski, C. W. Pollard, June Almes, Bettye Alexander, Michael Guest, and John O'Donnell, who read the earliest version. I'm grateful to them all. I especially thank Jeffrey Kerby, who read an early draft and reminded me why I was writing.

Agents Emma Sweeney and Justine Wenger saw the heart of the story and guided me early on, and Eldon Vaughan and G. K. Darby encouraged me. I'm grateful to Lawrence Knorr and everyone at Sunbury Press for making the book a reality.

I thank photographer Brad Loper for capturing striking images at Memorial and letting them grace our cover. Thanks also to photographer Terry Gaskins and to Amy Meaux, for technical assistance.

One person has accompanied me all the way in this writing venture, and in the process has become a fellow author and valued friend: Grace Frisone. Through draft after draft, I relied on Grace's careful reading, editorial comments, and unwavering confidence, and her humor, insight, and verve cheered me on. I thank her more than I can say.

Special thanks to Erin, who believed.

The joyful years I had with my husband Bob, his constant love, and his courage, dignity, and grace at the end were my inspiration. I'm glad I could tell at least part of his story. The line from Theodore Roethke's "The Waking" is true: *What falls away is always, and is near.*

SOURCES

Ashman, Howard (lyrics) and Alan Menken (music). "Beauty and the Beast." Walt Disney Music Company & Wonderland Music Company, 1991.

Auden, W. H. "Musée des Beaux Arts." W. H. Auden Collected Poems. Ed. Edward Mendelson. London: Faber and Faber, 1976. 146-147.

---. "Under Sirius." Mendelson 417-18.

Barry, John A. Rising Tide: The Great Mississippi Flood of 1927 and How It Changed America. New York: Simon & Schuster, 1997.

Deichmann, Richard E. Code Blue: A Katrina Physician's Memoir. Bloomington, IN: Rooftop, 2007.

Didion, Joan. The Year of Magical Thinking. New York: Vintage – Random House, 2006.

Eliot, T. S. "The Love Song of J. Alfred Prufrock." Collected Poems: 1909-1962. New York: Harcourt, 1963. 3-7.

---. "The Waste Land." Collected Poems: 1909-1962. 51-76.

Evans, G. Blakemore, ed. The Riverside Shakespeare. Boston: Houghton-Mifflin, 1974.

Goodman, Steve (music and lyrics). "City of New Orleans." Nancy Goodman-Tenny, Turnpike Tom Music, 1970.

MacDermot, Galt (music), James Rado, Gerome Ragni (lyrics). "Aquarius" from Hair. 1968.

"Make Me a Pallet on Your Floor." Traditional.

Meitrodt, Jeffrey. "For Dear Life: How Hope Turned to Despair at Memorial Medical Center." Parts 1-5. Times-Picayune 20-24 Aug. 2006: A1+

Newman, Randy (music and lyrics). "Louisiana 1927." Randy Newman, 1974.

Roethke, Theodore. "The Waking." The Collected Poems of Theodore Roethke. New York: Anchor-Doubleday, 1975. 104.

Shakespeare. King Lear. Evans, 1249-1305.

---. "Sonnet 66." Evans, 1761.

Williams, Tennessee. A Streetcar Named Desire. New York: Signet-New American Library, 1951.

---. Notebooks. Ed. Margaret Bradham Thornton. New Haven: Yale University Press, 2006.

Photo by Terry Gaskins

Carolyn Perry is the former director of the Writing Center at Lock Haven University in Pennsylvania, where she and her husband taught in the English Department. She lives in New Orleans.